# Caribbean Pilgrims

# Caribbean Pilgrims

## The Plight of the Haitian Refugees

## Daniel Dougé

AN EXPOSITION-UNIVERSITY BOOK

Exposition Press     Smithtown, New York

FIRST EDITION

© 1982 by Daniel Dougé

Library of Congress Catalog Card Number: 82-90274

ISBN 0-682-49890-4

Printed in the United States of America

To all the pilgrims of the world, with love

# Contents

*Introduction*                                               ix

1. The Elite within the Current Social Structure          1
2. The Sociological Role of Color Preferences             8
3. Language and Social Mobility                          24
4. The Foreign Influences                                35
5. What Happened to the Haitian Economy                  46
6. By Way of Conclusion                                  59

   *Notes*                                               63

   *Bibliography*                                        67

# Introduction

The "new" pilgrims were coming to the land of freedom and opportunity by small sailboats from one of the most economically depressed and politically oppressed countries in the Caribbean: Haiti.[1] Their mirage of hopeful socioeconomic development disappeared on the shores of Florida, while they drowned in the coastal waters, or upon their incarceration at various detention camps—the most notorious being the Krome Avenue detention center in Miami.

These Caribbean pilgrims missed Plymouth Rock by fifteen hundred miles and four centuries. Little did they know that the rug of hospitality would be pulled from underneath them and the gates of opportunity slammed shut in their black faces. Whereas, in their homeland, they were accustomed to welcoming American tourists; they themselves were now coming to America not as tourists, but as refugees without a penny or any skills, for the most part. Nevertheless, even though they did not expect a welcoming committee, they only hoped for the chance to earn a living by the sweat of their brows. If only they knew that, as black refugees from a nation that was long considered an outcast in international circles, they would not be entitled to the same treatment as other refugees.

The ill-informed refugees lacked the awareness of the fear and, in many cases, the virulent hatred nurtured by many Americans who want to preserve their genetic heritage and protect the land and resources that their ancestors conquered from the "Indians." Indeed, they were ignorant of the great fear of miscegenation suffered by these Americans who themselves descended from people who migrated to this land under similar circumstances.

The fear of miscegenation, the fear of being overwhelmed by nonwhites, is a very important concern of white America. But, on the contrary, it is the rest of the world that should harbor such fears. World history clearly shows that it is European peoples who expanded and settled on all the continents of the globe at the expense of the native populations, which, in many instances are near extinction or became extinct as a direct result of that settlement. However, the whites' fear of nonwhites has persisted as a psychological and cultural complex. That is why racist organizations such as the KKK, the American Nazi Party, and the like have flourished in a country whose ideals are that all men are created equal.

So, the Caribbean pilgrims fell victim to their ignorance and their naive faith—victim to their desperate hope that somehow they would find some human kindness and generosity in a country that their ancestors had helped fight for independence. They lacked the awareness that their very humanity was denied by segments of the population and, consequently, unworthy of sympathy and compassion.

What shattered hopes for a people who craved so much for freedom and found it denied both at home and abroad. What appeals could be made when those who attend the churches and temples of the land hear but ignore the message of universal love and brotherhood, or when that message is interpreted to exclude nonwhites? What can be done when those to whom these refugees could appeal for aid are themselves involved in perpetuating the very conditions of their desperation? If that is not hell, what is? Yet, these execrable conditions, while they might well lead to their extinction, might also turn into the crucible of a newly born awareness, namely that they must find within themselves the solace and the courage to survive, to live and create their happiness wherever they are on their own.

The timing of the Haitian refugees could not have been any worse. They were seeking asylum in the United States during a period of economic recession, increased racial tensions, and a heightened fear of communist aggression. In addition, the United States government was plagued by large budget deficits and was under pressure to cut spending as well as taxes. As bad as these conditions seemed to self-preoccupied Americans at home, they still did not compare to the plight of the Haitian refugees who could do little to influence the political and economic pressures that forced them to seek a better future for themselves outside of their homeland. These were people who had sacrificed all they had just to pay for a perilous sea voyage in overcrowded sailboats with whatever food and water they could carry to last the duration of the trip. These were people whose bodies washed ashore like the carcasses of dead whales because they could not complete the last leg of their journey as they were forced to swim to the beaches of Miami by boat captains who feared arrest by the American authorities.

Obviously, if living conditions were better, Haitians would never leave their beloved country under such humiliating circumstances. The problems that they faced had been brewing for decades, if not centuries. Haitians had long been migrating to Cuba before Castro came into power and to the Dominican Republic where they worked primarily as sugarcane cutters. Nassau was also another refuge for many of them. It was not until the late 1970s that the United States, and in particular south Florida, became flooded with illegal Haitian immigrants. Though Haitians had for years legally migrated to the United States of America, their immigration here had never before taken this form.

What exactly were the conditions that led to the arrival of these unwanted black refugees? The general American public knows Haiti as the country formerly ruled by a dictator called "Papa Doc," and now by his son "Baby Doc." It knows about the *tontons macoute,* or civil militia, which is feared by most Haitians. It is also aware that Haiti is a poor country, but that it is also a beautiful land where tourists go to enjoy its sun, mountains, beaches, and its generally hospitable culture. However, beyond this superficial aspect, to merely describe in greater details the current conditions is simply to view the tip of the iceberg. The understanding of current conditions requires a historical analysis of the problems that plague the country. Besides the broad historical perspective, sociological, political and economic factors should be analyzed as well. We have to look beyond the symptoms to the cause of the problems that have led to this exodus of refugees.

The first place to look is at the leadership of Haiti, for its leaders bear ultimate responsibility for the living conditions in the country. By leadership is meant not only the political leaders, but the whole class of people constituting the elite of the society. These were the people who were entrusted, or took upon themselves, the responsibility to lead the country politically, culturally, and economically. This analysis will reveal the fabric of the Haitian social structure and allow the identification of the refugees' socioeconomic background. As poor as the country may be, a significant segment of its elite enjoy untold comfort and luxury by any Western standards.

Although Haitian society may appear free of prejudice to a casual outside observer, color preferences inherited from its colonial past significantly affect the mobility of its members. Such preferences, which could be taken lightly, have had tangible economic and political consequences for all Haitians. The consequences were favorable for those beneficially affected and deleterious to those victimized. It is interesting to see how a society continued to be afflicted with a social problem of colonial origin even after more than 175 years of independence.

Another factor that has similarly affected social mobility and development, in general, in the country is its linguistic situation. Here is a nation that for years maintained as its official means of communication a language that 80 percent to 90 percent of its population could not understand. It is obvious that the speakers of the official language, French, enjoyed many benefits that were denied the illiterate masses who spoke only Creole.

In addition to its internal problems, international influences also account for existing conditions. By virtue of its strategic location, size, and its history, Haiti was subject to the attention of many foreign powers. And even with some of the latter's best intentions, the country lost more than it gained in its relations with them.

All the above factors contribute to the sorry state of the Haitian economy. Haiti never again experienced the prosperity of colonial times. The restructuring of the labor supply in its agriculturally based economy geared toward the production of cash crops for export, while it provided greater political freedom to the population, failed to generate national economic development. Consequently, the restructuring stunted the political and social evolution of its people.

It is through the analyses of these various factors that the current Haitian situation should be understood. The recent waves of Haitian refugees on the shores of Florida were the symptoms of these deeper problems. Those who are sincerely interested in finding true solutions to the Haitian problem will be better apprised of what needs to be done. It should also be evident how a small nation such as Haiti and its relatively small number of refugees became a political football in the West vs. East game, while the harsher realities of hunger, disease, illiteracy, poverty, and political oppression were ignored or even justified by those powers that could truly help.

The warm and sandy beaches of south Florida were certainly no Plymouth Rock. No "Indians" came to the rescue of these starving and freedom-loving Caribbean pilgrims. Yet, those who survived and were released from their prisons will still celebrate Thanksgiving together with the rest of the American population, if not with turkey, they will perhaps be grateful to enjoy some chicken earned by the sweat of their brows.

# *Caribbean Pilgrims*

# 1

# The Elite within the Current Social Structure

The term elite is so familiar that it is conceptually vague. Social scientists who used it in their analyses of societies failed to be any more consistent with its usage than ordinary folk. They disagreed on its precise meaning, usage, and usefulness. Even the dictionary definition lacked precision: "the choice part; especially a socially superior group; a powerful minority group."[1] Elite then referred to a certain definable group of people in qualitative terms: socially superior and powerful minority. How could a socially superior group be determined objectively? What constituted social superiority? Superior is a relative term that implies a value judgment. What is meant by powerful minority? How is power to be measured? Is it economic power, political power, military power, or what else? People in a group or in society at large occupy positions of relative power with respect to one another. Some persons or groups of persons wield more power than others. The problem is to determine which of these groups constituted the elite.

Various types of elite were mentioned in analyses of social stratification: intellectual, rural, military, etc. They all involved the notion that a certain group of people was in some manner or other better than or superior to the other people in their environment. What exactly made such individuals superior to others would naturally depend upon the evaluation criteria

1

chosen. Were such people identified as members of an elite on account of their reputation, their income, their character, or their personal achievements? Since the criteria for membership in an elite are not given by definition, they will have to be delineated before the actual group of people in question can be identified.

Various terms have been used to designate the dominant segment of Haitian society. James G. Leyburn called it an elite caste. He viewed the society as divided into two castes: the elite and the masses. His use of the term "caste" was inappropriate. He conducted his study, *The Haitian People,* not long after the American Occupation, which lasted from 1915 to 1934. The American forces had perpetrated a certain amount of racism during their stay in the country. They exacerbated the prejudices that were already extant in Haitian society. The gap between the elite and the masses had widened in the process. What he observed during the first half of the 1940s was the temporary effects of the Occupation. The clique of Haitians that the Occupation forces had brought to power exhibited then the ostensible characteristics of a caste. This clique lost the reins of power in 1946.

> The Social Revolution of 1946 was the culmination of the nationalist movement led by Haitian intellectuals during the American Occupation and which was accelerated by World War II. This date marks the accession to power of a non-mulatto and non-bourgeois government. It resulted in better employment, education, and other social opportunities for the other classes and a general "defrosting" of the rigid class system. It is also a refutation of the imitative French culture imposed on the nation by the mulatto bourgeoisie. From then on interest was focused on discovering the long-neglected Haitian cultural heritage which led to a renewed interest in the African roots of Haiti.[2]

A more recent study of Haiti's social structure was conducted by R. Wingfield and V. J. Parenton in *Class Structure and Class Conflict in Haitian Society.* The social divisions that were designated in this analysis were as follows: traditional bourgeoisie, middle class, urban proletariat, and peasant mass. The new terminology is immediately noticeable. The proliferation of terms to designate the various social classes could lead to confusion. The traditional bourgeoisie corresponded to Leyburn's elite caste. Bourgeoisie and elite were often used interchangeably to refer to Haitians who occupied the upper class. It is also interesting to note that although bourgeoisie and middle class could be considered synonymous, they did not designate the same group of people in analyses of Haiti's social structure. The distinction between these two terms in Haiti's case was that the bourgeoisie contained the long-established families of Haiti's upper class, especially the descendants of the freedmen, whereas middle class designated the upwardly mobile elements on the periphery of the bourgeoisie. The dominant social class was also called an aristocracy. In fact, Leyburn referred to the members of his elite caste as aristocrats and aristocratic.[3] To add to the confusion, J. Price-Mars added to this already long list of terms the expression "middle-class elite."[4]

Elite, bourgeoisie, middle class, and aristocracy were the various terms used to refer to the dominant segment or segments of Haitian society. In general, the people referred to as elite constituted a rather ill-defined group. Its members were presumably few in numbers and dominated socially, economically, and politically. The bourgeoisie comprised people particularly involved in business.[5] While the definition of middle class overlapped with that of bourgeoisie, the first referred specifically to the socioeconomic stratum located between an upper class and a lower class. The distinction that was made in the Haitian situation was justified because the bourgeoisie was regarded as the upper class. Aristocracy means "a government in which power is vested in a minority consisting of those felt to be superior."[6] Both elite and aristocracy carried the notions of power and superiority, whereas bourgeoisie and middle class stressed the economic stance of the people involved. Whatever the terms used, all the structural analyses conveyed the idea that there existed in Haiti a small group of people who had monopolized the privileges, wealth, power, and prestige present in the society.

Leyburn's binary partition of Haitian society contrasted with Wingfield and Parenton's analysis, which identified four separate social classes. Other studies divided the society into three classes: upper class, middle class, and lower class. The problem confronted by all the structural analyses was that the upper class and middle class of Haiti were not economically differentiated as well as those in highly industrialized societies. The relatively small commercial sector was dominated by the members of the upper class and by foreigners or naturalized aliens. No substantial industrial sector existed in the economy.

It was impossible to rigorously differentiate the social strata of Haiti on an economic basis alone. A whole other set of factors entered into their total configuration. "Illimitable social distances between elite and mass, as well as inescapable social nearnesses, are occasioned by objective differences in language, occupations, religion, recreation, family life, income, education, mobility, and political power, and by the internalization of the ideal patterns associated with these dissimilarities."[7] For instance, a Haitian could be considered a member of the bourgeoisie by virtue of his parentage and education alone; wealth and power were more a function of whomever occupied the presidential palace.

The social structure derived by Wingfield and Parenton best fit the current Haitian social reality. The bourgeoisie consisted of those few families that descended from the freedmen of Saint-Domingue and included the foreigners who came to do business in the country. The members of this class were found in the government, when political conditions were favorable, and in the professions and commerce. They also owned large properties. The middle class, also known as the petty bourgeoisie, was made up of upwardly mobile people who remained peripheral to the bourgeoisie until they could gain acceptance either through intermarriage or some other means. Political power and wealth helped but did not guarantee entry into the bourgeoisie. Members of the middle class also occupied government positions under favorable political conditions. They were commonly found in the civil service and the professions. Their ranks also included traders and wealthy farmers. The urban proletariat comprised the people employed by light industry, tradesmen, house servants, manual laborers, and all the unemployed migrants from the rural areas who settled in the towns and cities. The peasantry encompassed the rural population, which was chiefly involved in subsistence farming and the cultivation of crops for export.

The hierarchical structure of Haitian society will be bisected horizontally for our analytical purposes. Two larger and more inclusive concepts will constitute the principal analytical categories. The two main social divisions will be classified as the elite and the masses. The elite, as conceived here, will comprise both the bourgeoisie and the middle class. These strata of Haitian society possessed certain common characteristics that set them apart from the rest of the society. In the main, their members were educated and took turns governing the country. The urban proletariat kept many features of the peasantry whence it came. It shared the latter's illiteracy and powerlessness. It is, therefore, amalgamated to the peasantry, and together they will be considered as the masses.

Two other synonymous concepts, "ruling class" and "leadership," could have been used to designate the dominant social segment. However, the term elite encompassed these concepts, and more. S. F. Nadel's definition suited well our usage of it in the Haitian social context:

> An elite is not simply coterminous with high status and a superior position somehow shared by a body of people; neither does it necessarily coincide with a fully organized and "closed" group. In other words, elites, as here understood, must have some degree of corporateness, good character, and exclusiveness. There must be barriers to admission. The people said to form an elite must be aware of their preeminent position and all that it entails as something which they enjoy jointly and which sets them off from other people; which means, they must form a more or less self-conscious unit within the society. . . .[8]

Our special use of the term does not preclude any other possible usage. Mercier's definition remained just as valid: "Whoever possesses a sufficient level of intellectual culture, certain qualities of character, or instead, strong enough traditions, a certain upbringing, gladly considers himself a man of elite."[9] Dr. François Duvalier (1907-1971), who was from the middle class, thought of elite as a title that was bestowed only upon the residents of fashionable districts, certain families for the most part tinged with classical culture, especially those who thought of the Republic as their own patrimony.[10] Regardless of these other definitions, the elite must be viewed within the context of our structural analysis in contrast to the masses, that is, the bourgeoisie and the middle class versus the urban proletariat and the peasantry.

The definition of the Haitian elite as including the members of both the middle class and the bourgeoisie implied that the conflicts between these two groups would have to be viewed as an internal struggle within a single social class. As already indicated, both groups shared the same education and similar cultural values, and their members all aspired to the same political and economic roles that they in fact shared. The internal conflicts of the elite stemmed from the acute competition among its members for political and economic gains, and from color prejudice. It is the latter factor that divided the members of this class into two antagonistic factions. The subject of color prejudice will be fully explored in the following chapter.

The primary concern of the elite was status. It disdained the trades and manual labor. Its members favored the professions and politics; they encouraged their children to become medical doctors, engineers, and lawyers regardless of their individual preferences and abilities. They were uninterested in agriculture, the mainstay of the economy. Most wanted to enrich themselves without devoting their personal efforts and capital to the development of industry. Instead, they preferred to speculate in the commercial sector where quick and substantial profits could be made and stashed away in domestic and foreign banks as protection against the political instability that they themselves created. Their general attitudes and values filtered down to the rest of the society, undermined the leadership that they provided the country, and hurt national interests.

The lack of opportunities for upward mobility by members of the masses worsened their living conditions. The elite monopolized the single most important means of social advancement: education. The lack of education deprived people of a knowledge of the official language and severely impeded the flow of ideas that might have fostered national development. President François Duvalier (1957-1971), "Papa Doc," used political means to relieve and check the socioeconomic pressures on the masses. He established the *tontons macoute* as a civil militia both to protect his administration and to provide a channel for upward mobility for his supporters. His draconian methods only provided partial and temporary relief through the displacement of members of the elite. In general, the elite stymied economic growth by its incessant internal struggles for the spoils of political power. It bankrupted the government and the country. Haiti needed a stable, organized, and dedicated leadership, which was concerned with the national interest, to resolve its problems and promote its development.

# 2

# The Sociological Role
# of Color Preferences

During the seventeenth and eighteenth century, the colonial situation in Saint-Domingue was similar to that of many other places in the world. The colony was divided into two camps: the white and the nonwhite. Its political structure consisted in the subjugation of the nonwhites by the whites under the hegemony of a metropolitan administration. It was a forced labor camp where nonwhite labor was exploited on expropriated lands for the benefit of the colonists and their metropolis. Social relations between the two groups were deeply affected by racism.[1]

The cornerstone of colonial ideology was the presumed inherent superiority of European peoples and their cultures against the presumed inferiority of the subjugated non-European and nonwhite world. It were as if the colonial world were inhabited by two different species of human beings.[2] Sartre expressed it in this fashion: "Not so very long ago, the earth numbered two thousand million inhabitants: five hundred million men, and one thousand five hundred million natives."[3]

A racial and color hierarchy existed in Saint-Domingue following the political and economic structure of the colony. The decreasing order of dominance went from white to mulatto to black. This corresponded roughly to the colonists, the freedmen and the slaves. People of mixed ancestry were numerically preponderant in the class of freedmen.

Although the people of African and European ancestry were commonly called mulattoes, a sophisticated vocabulary was developed to designate them. This further attested to the importance given to race and color in Saint-Domingue:[4]

|  *Mates* | *Offsprings* |
|---|---|
| white man + black African Woman | = mulatto |
| "        "        + mulatto woman | = quadroon |
| "        "        + quadroon woman | = "mamelouc" |
| "        "        + "mamelouc" woman | = "quarteronné" |
| "        "        + "quarteronné" woman | = mixed-blood |
| "        "        + mixed-blood woman | = mixed-blood |
| black man + mulatto woman | = "griffe" |
| "        "        + "griffe" woman | = "sacatra" |
| "        "        + "quarteronné" woman | = "marabou" |
| "        "        + "marabou" woman | = "sacatra" |

The scarcity of white women in the colony provided added stimulus to the union of Europeans and Africans. However, even the colonist who had a white woman to himself was likely to indulge in sex with a slave of his choice. They often picked their mates from their domestic slaves. The house servants consequently tended to become increasingly lighter in complexion over the generations.

Membership into the freedmen class was determined by the system of manumission. Certain colonists manumitted the slaves who gained their favor or otherwise bought their freedom. They freed their mulatto offsprings more frequently than the other black slaves. Some black women desired children by their white masters because such children stood a greater chance of being manumitted.

Other than color, there were various criteria of status among the slaves. Creole slaves, those born in the colony, felt superior to the new arrivals from Africa. Educated and skilled slaves enjoyed a higher status than their brethren. The black slave overseers obviously occupied a higher position than their peers. The medicine men and religious leaders were also accorded prestige, and so were the traditional African chiefs and their descendants. Lastly, the domestic slaves harbored feelings of superiority toward those in the fields on account of their proximity to the masters.

Indeed, the total value of the nonwhites in the colony depended upon their cultural and genetic closeness to the whites. The white, colonial upper class was the model that the freedmen and the slaves sought to emulate in every respect. Race and color were by far the most important measure of status. Even mulatto slaves felt superior to free black persons on account of their white parentage. The colonial, racial ideology relegated blacks to the most inferior or subhuman status. The enslaved blacks lost much of their cultural heritage, their African identity, and their human dignity after a number of generations under these conditions. All that remained for them and everybody else as a model of a free and dignified human being was the white colonist.

The slaves and the freedmen founded the nation of Haiti in 1804. The psychological problems that originated from the colonial system were inherited by the new state. The past colonial experience could not be totally expunged from the Haitian consciousness by the successful war of independence and the expulsion of the colonists. The resulting social and psychological pathologies continued to plague contemporary Haitian society down to the present.

Although the rigid color bar of colonial times was not maintained in Haitian society, color still played an important role. The following Haitian expression described well the new situation: "A rich black is a mulatto; a poor mulatto is black." The paradoxical nature of this statement underlined the socioeconomic status that went with being black or mulatto. Black was associated with poverty and low class, and mulatto with the opposite. While both blacks and mulattoes were found throughout the social structure of Haiti, mulattoes predominated in the elite. In that respect, not much was changed from colonial times.

Color prejudice was one of the important problems that Haiti faced since its independence. Dessalines, the founding father of the nation, was quite aware of this. He decreed that all Haitians were to be known as blacks regardless of the color of their skin. This superficial remedy failed to resolve this social issue that had both aesthetic and politico-economic implications. Haitian social relations remained racist in character long after the colonial experience. People continued to give social significance to the differences in physical features and skin color insofar as they measured up to the white European phenotype. They had adopted the somatic norm image of their former European masters. (Harry Hoetink defined the "somatic norm image" as the complex of physical characteristics that were accepted by a group as its standard of beauty.[5])

The European somatic norm image became that of the Haitian population through its past colonial experience. Hoetink explained the process simply as follows: "In a society in which the somatic norm image of the dominant segment $A$ is completely different from that of the subordinate segment $B$, segment $B$ will, assuming that the social order of the segments is constant, take over the somatic norm image of segment $A$."[6] Obviously, in Saint-Domingue, segment $A$ consisted of the white colonists; and segment $B$, the freedmen and the slaves.

Colonial society created the psychological conditions under which the subjugated population was forced to view and accept the colonists' aesthetic values as superior; the transference of the somatic norm image was a one-way process brought about by a number of generations of actual subordination on the basis of cultural differences.[7] The form of slavery that was instituted by the colonists literally transformed the Africans into beasts of burden. They were dehumanized. In their quest to maintain some human dignity and to escape their immediate condition psychologically, they identified with their masters. They wanted to enjoy their privileges and to be white as well, because it was clear to them that one had to be white in order to have freedom, dignity, power, wealth, and beauty in the white, colonial world.

What caused the transference of the somatic norm image of the whites to the nonwhites was more than just psychological in nature. The colonial order was maintained by brute force. Segregation and the colonial forms of social etiquette were enforced physically; severe corporal punishments were administered to the blacks who violated the rules governing their relations with the whites.

The imposition of the European somatic norm image produced certain psychological pathologies in the non-European population, namely an inferiority complex and self-hatred. These problems resulted from the victims' non-fulfillment of their own somatic norm image. Haitians continued to suffer from a collective sense of non-fulfillment of their somatic norm image because their society inadvertently remained pathological.[8] Since the transference of the somatic norm image was essentially a sociocultural phenomenon, the aesthetic values upheld by the society were passed on to its members during the course of their socialization. These psychological problems, which originated from the colonial experience, were thus perpetuated from generation to generation through the normal transmission of the pathological cultural values that caused them.

According to Hoetink, once the adoption of the dominant somatic norm image became a fact, the society would continue to have a "race problem" between whites and blacks despite the absence of the dominant segment.[9] He contended that Haiti constituted a good illustration of his argument.[10] The evidence did seem to support his analysis. Colonial racism still affected the society internally even though its members were no longer colonized. Haitians had internalized the French, colonial racist values that fostered color prejudice and made them prey to self-hatred and a complex of inferiority.

Given that color prejudice was a racial problem, sociological models of race relations could certainly apply to the Haitian situation. Pierre L. Van Den Berghe contended that manifestations of racial prejudice were historically polarized around two ideal-types: the paternalistic and competitive types.[11] The paternalistic type will be examined to evaluate the social situation in Haiti. Although it would be equally interesting to see how this typological model applied to Saint-Domingue, contemporary Haitian society will constitute the primary subject as the focus of this study. The paternalistic model was chosen because the competitive ideal-type was by definition compatible with a complex manufacturing economy and with large-scale industrial capitalism, neither of which Haiti possessed. What also influenced the choice of Van Den Berghe's typology was his claim that his ideal-types could apply *mutatis mutandis* to forms of prejudice other than racial.[12] His typology could therefore be used to analyze Haitian social relations even though distinct racial groups no longer existed within the native population (there was a small foreign white population in the country).

For fear of putting undue emphasis on the racial aspect of the problem, one might insist that color prejudice rather than racial bigotry was the affliction in question. However, the difference between the two is really academic. The person, black or white, who shows contempt for blackness expresses not only color prejudice but also racial prejudice since his bias would affect all black people in general. The black person who is affected by self-hatred and wishes to be something other than what he is expresses not just color prejudice but racial prejudice as well.

Here is how Van Den Berghe's ideal-type of paternalistic race relations will be used in the analysis: his categories for the ideal-type will be enumerated as given in his study, *Race and Ethnicity,* Table 1-1, but each category will be commented upon and compared to the Haitian situation, and, as already discussed in the previous chapter, Haitian society will be viewed as divided into two major classes: the elite and the masses.

The danger presented by a simplistic typological approach is that it can easily lead to prejudice, especially when its purpose is to affix a permanent label on entities or processes that are constantly subject to change and to wide individual differentiation. This analysis is conducted strictly to determine the extent to which Haitian society retained the characteristics of the antecedent colonial system. The typology and the following comparative analysis will serve no other goals beyond this stated purpose.

Pierre L. Van Den Berghe, in Table 1-1,* gave the following three sets of variables:[13]

## A.  INDEPENDENT VARIABLES

1. *Economy*: Nonmanufacturing, agricultural, pastoral, handicraft; mercantile capitalism; plantation economy.

The Haitian economy was evidently of the type mentioned here. It was basically agricultural and followed the colonial pattern whereby raw materials and agricultural crops were exchanged for manufactured consumer goods.

2. *Division of labor*: Simple (primitive) or intermediate (as in preindustrial large-scale societies). Division of labor along racial lines. Wide income gap between racial groups.

The occupational differences between the elite and the masses, namely managerial, professional, administrative, and clerical positions versus manual and menial work, corresponded roughly to the prevailing color differences between the members of these two classes. They also resulted in a significant income gap between the two groups.

3. *Mobility*: Little mobility either vertical or horizontal (slaves, servants, or serfs "attached" in space).

When George E. Simpson made his study of Haiti's social structure in 1941, he found that the Haitian population tended to be spatially immobile. This was especially true of the peasants. The members of the elite had greater mobility than the latter.[14] The political mobilization of the rural and urban populations under the Duvalier regime changed this. As a result, rural migration to the cities and towns was stimulated. But although there was a great deal

*From *Race and Ethnicity: Essays in Comparative Sociology,* by Pierre L. Van Den Berghe. © 1970 by Basic Books, Inc. Used by permission.

more mobility in contemporary Haitian society, vertical mobility remained the prerogative of the few.

Slaves or serfs did not legally exist in Haiti. Instead, there were peasants, wage laborers, and "domestiques." The latter could be viewed as domestic slaves; however, the context of their servitude differed from the colonial one. Their position resulted from the economic conditions that prevailed in the country. Because they were unable to provide for them, certain poor Haitians placed their children at the homes of better-off families, sometimes distant relatives of theirs. Such children were expected to perform domestic work in exchange for room and board, and some schooling if they were lucky. The domestiques were usually treated like the maids or worse. On the other hand, many people treated them well. The domestiques were free to leave any time their parents wanted them back or whenever they became old enough to support themselves.

4. *Social stratification*:  Caste system with horizontal color bar. Aristocracy vs. servile caste with wide gap in living standards (as indexed by income, education, death and birth rates). Homogeneous upper caste.

Whereas the Haitian elite might be compared to an aristocracy, the masses of Haiti did not constitute a servile caste. A caste system did not exist and there was no rigid color bar. Color prejudice constituted an obstacle that could be overcome, to an extent, through education and the acquisition of wealth and power. The lack of economic and educational opportunities for the masses rendered the social structure somewhat inflexible.

The living standards of the two groups differed greatly. The masses generally lived at the subsistence level, were illiterate, and lacked access to good medical care. The schools and the hospitals were concentrated in the important urban centers where the elite resided. The elite was homogenous insofar as its members shared the same outlook on life, a similar education, and similar aspirations.

5. *Numerical ratio*:   Dominant group a small minority.

Various estimates placed the rural population of Haiti between 80 percent and 90 percent, leaving 20 percent to 10 percent of the total population in the urban areas. Since the urban proletariat would be subtracted from the urban population, the Haitian elite probably constituted less than 10 percent of the country's total population.

6. *Value conflict*:   Integrated value system. No ideological conflict.

The elite and the masses lived in two different worlds. The members of the elite led a westernized way of life. The urban proletariat also shared this world though to a lesser extent. The contrast was greater in the case of the peasantry. The peasants were the carriers of the national culture. The members of the elite were proud to be among the few bearers of French culture in this hemisphere.[15]

While the isolated and uneducated rural populations observed their own folkloric traditions, they still aspired to the life of the elite. Consequently, the whole society was oriented toward French culture. This orientation was reinforced by the official language (French) and the French educational system adopted by the country. Nevertheless, a measure of ideological conflict existed between the Francophile and nationalistic forces. This conflict was apparent in twentieth-century Haitian literature. For instance, the nationalistic movement of *Les Griots,* in which Dr. François Duvalier participated, conflicted with the ideology of people like Dantes Bellegarde, a staunch supporter of French culture.

B. DEPENDENT VARIABLES

1. *Race relations*:   Accommodation. Everyone is in his place and "knows it." Paternalism. Benevolent despotism.

*Social relations between classes* should replace the terms *race relations* in this variable. Haitian social classes were accommodated to one another because most Haitians were fatalistic about their station in life. While the elite appeared paternalistic, the self-hatred that afflicted it led to the worst kinds of despotism.

2. *Roles and status:* Sharply defined roles and status based on ascription, particularism, diffuseness, collectivity orientation, affectivity. Unequal status unthreatened.

All the cultural, educational, and occupational differences between the classes served to determine the role and status of Haitians. Since the members of the social classes did not enjoy equal opportunities, role and status were determined by birth rather than personal achievement. The masses viewed the world of the elite as something that was largely beyond their reach. Since the elite also monopolized the primary means of social mobility; i.e., education, wealth and political power, the social structure of the country suffered no major threats from the masses.

3. *Etiquette:* Elaborate and definite.

Haitian etiquette was fairly elaborate and definite, and it evolved from the French colonial code of conduct. It helped maintain the social distance between the elite and the masses despite the close contact of their members.

4. *Forms of aggression:* Generally from lower caste: slave rebellions, nationalistic, revivalistic, or messianic movements. Not directly racial. "Righteous" punishment from the master.

Haiti was an independent state that had long overthrown its colonial regime. While the masses revolted against the elite, all the revolutions since independence resulted, for the most part, from power struggles within the elite itself.

However, color prejudice was implicated in the conflicts that set apart various factions of the elite. The notion of "righteous" punishment from the master did not apply.

5. *Miscegenation*:   Condoned and frequent between upper-caste males and lower-caste females. Institutionalized concubinage.

Sexual relations between classes were frequent. They usually involved upper-class males and lower-class females. The women of the elite remained secluded from lower-class males. Intermarriage between the classes was discouraged; these infrequent unions usually involved an upwardly mobile member of the lower-class with the necessary wealth and power to secure such an alliance. Concubinage was institutionalized; these relationships were likely to remain clandestine when they involved members of the elite.

6. *Segregation*:   Little of it. Status gap allows close but unequal contact.

Segregation was absent. Yet, the elite and the masses still lived in two practically separate worlds. There was a great deal of contact between the members of the elite and the masses. These contacts were restricted to situations where roles and status were not threatened. They also resided in different areas, primarily due to economic reasons. Most elite social functions took place in a private context such that uninvited guests were unlikely to intrude. Both the elite and the masses shared the use of all public places and utilities equally.

7. *Psychological syndrome*:   Internalized subservient status. No personality "need" for prejudice. No high F. Pseudo tolerance.

If Van Den Berghe had taken account of the one-way transference of the somatic norm image of the whites to the blacks, he would have had to mention the resulting self-hatred. He also would have detected that there existed at least a subconscious personality "need" for prejudice due to the related complex of inferiority at the root of the Haitians' color prejudice. "The Negro is comparison. There is the first truth. He is comparison: that is, he is constantly preoccupied with self-evaluation and with the ego-ideal. Whenever he comes into contact with someone else, the question of value, of merit, arises."[16]

Haitians inherited the traits of passive obedience and submission to authority from their colonial past and from years of brutal political tyranny by the country's dictatorial governments. These traits were reinforced by the socialization process; parental tyranny was also common in many Haitian families. Parents enjoyed absolute authority over their children, whom they often bent to their will by physical coercion. One might say that the whole society was pseudo-tolerant because its members harbored pent-up aggression as a result of its authoritarian nature.

8. *Stereotypes of lower caste*:   Childish, immature, exuberant, uninhibited, lazy, impulsive, fun-loving, good-humored. Inferior but lovable.

The stereotypes of the masses presumably approximated those given above. This inference was made from the observed general attitudes of the elite toward the masses. The latter were considered inferior but not lovable. The elite had contempt for them, a manifestation of its own self-hatred and complex of inferiority.

9. *Intensity of prejudice*:   Fairly constant.

The intensity of color prejudice was fairly constant in Haiti on account of the relative stability of the social structure.

## C.   SOCIAL CONTROL VARIABLES

1. *Form of government*:   Aristocratic, oligarchic, autocratic. Either centralized or feudal. Colonial.

All the types of government mentioned above corre-
spond to those that Haiti experienced throughout its history.
The governments were essentially dictatorial and very centralized.

2. *Legal system*:  Lower caste has separate legal status.
   Law on side of racial status quo. Weber's traditional
   type of authority.

Haitian law recognized as citizens all persons born of
Haitian parents in the country. While the legal system provided separate codes for the urban and rural populations,
roughly the elite versus the masses, it did not recognize
any social classes and did not sanction the color differences
among people. All Haitians, regardless of how they looked,
were legally black. The law, in general, had a very limited
role in this authoritarian society. Those who occupied positions of authority were the law. Their power was absolute
unless it could be superceded by someone else from above
in the political structure.

This last variable concludes Van Den Berghe's ideal-
type of paternalistic race relations.

It is evident from the preceding discussion that only superficial changes would be required to make this model fit the
Haitian pattern of social relations. The majority of changes would
involve the substitution of terms such as "color" for "race,"
"class" for "caste," "elite" for "aristocracy," and "masses" for
"servile caste." Other modifications would be required by independent variables 3. and 4. due to the political structure and
status of Haiti. Independent variable 6. would be altered to
acknowledge the presence of ideological conflict. Dependent
variable 4. would necessitate a greater degree of modification
because of its strong colonial flavor. Substantial changes would
also be needed at dependent variables 1. and 7. due to the
integration of Hoetink's and Fanon's theses in the analysis. In
summary, from a grand total of seventeen variables, three would
require major changes; and only three others, minor alterations.

The ready adaptation of Van Den Berghe's colonial model of race relations to Haitian social relations demonstrated the degree to which Haitian society retained a colonial character.[17] Color prejudice was only one of the indexes that pointed to this fact.

The French educational system adopted by the country contributed to the problem, perhaps unintentionally. Except for Haitian history and literature, virtually all the books used were written by French authors who were naturally interested in propagating French culture and the French somatic norm image through pictorial and literary descriptions; these books were written for French students. The emphasis on learning by rote forced the acceptance of the French values, which did not reflect the Haitian cultural environment. The educational system was designed to produce graduates with a formation equivalent, if not identical, to that which would be received in French schools. This result was achieved at the cost of the total psychocultural alienation of Haitian students who learned to value French culture at the expense of their own. The national culture became viewed as the manifestation of a largely ignorant, uncivilized, inferior, and shameful world. Students failed to gain a positive appreciation of their blackness to the point where it was an insult to be called black. The negative values associated with blackness were embodied in the French language itself:

> **Black**—adjective (Latin *niger*). Designates the darkest color produced by the absence of light; also designates objects of this color: *black hair.*// That which is of a dark color: *black bread.*// Dark: *black night.*// Bruised: *black-and-blue from bruises.*// Dirty, filthy: *black hands.*// Sad, gloomy: *black ideas.*// Wicked, evil: *black soul.* \*\*\* *"Bête noire"* or *black beast*—French expression also used in English—a person or thing usually strongly and persistently detested, feared, or avoided.// *Black funds:* slush funds.// *Black body* (Physics), body which absorbs all light.// *To be black* (Vernacular), to be drunk.// *Black market,* trading activity in violation of public regulations.// *Black mass,* mass celebrated in honor of an evil power.// *Black novel, film,* whose plot conveys pessimism.//—Noun. Person who belongs to the black race.//—Masculine noun. Black color: *jet-black.*// Black cloth, clothing or color of mourning: *to wear black* meaning

to be in mourning.// In the military, center of shooting target: *to hit in the black.* \*\*\* *To be in a black mood,* to be preoccupied with gloomy reflections.// *Black indigo,* coloring agent.// *Bone-black,* animal charcoal.// *Lampblack,* industrial pigment produced by carbon particles.// *Black pocket,* gland of cephalopods secreting dark liquid when in flight.// *To see everything in black,* to take a gloomy view of everything.//—Adverb. In black: *to paint black.*[18]

White represented the opposite:

**White**—adjective (borrowed from German). Color of milk and snow.// Light color: *white wine.*// That which is not dirty: *white linen.*//—*Figuratively.* Innocent: *white as snow.* \*\*\* *White weapon,* weapon used for cutting or stabbing.// *White water,* acetate solution used for sprains, burns, etc.// *White sore,* whitlow, inflammation or infection near nails of fingers or toes.// *White metal,* metal alloy resembling silver.// *White night,* sleepless night.// *White paper,* blank paper.// *White fathers,* missionary group founded by Cardinal Lavigerie in Africa.// *White sauce,* sauce made from butter and flour, without coloration.// *White verse,* free verse.// *White voice,* lacking in tone.//—Noun. Person belonging to the white race: *the Whites.* (Capitalized as a proper name.)[19]

So, Haitians were taught to hate themselves.

The existence of color prejudice in the society always put in question the self-esteem of Haitians. They doubted their self-worth, as they evaluated themselves and one another by the external trappings that were supposed to give them a measure of dignity—the dignity that their forefathers lost in the colonial experience. They lacked an awareness of the psychological consequences of the traumatic, colonial experience and were reluctant to admit to themselves and others that they suffered from an inferiority complex. There was a need to compensate for their psychological feelings of inadequacy in all their activities.

Color prejudice was a key factor responsible for undermining the social and economic evolution of the country. The principal way in which it affected national development was through the ineffective usage of human resources. It constituted an internal force of disunity that hampered the formation of viable socio-political institutions. It produced conflicts both between and within the social classes. The social revolution of 1946 and Duvalier's revolution in 1957, for instance, essentially involved political struggles between the black and mulatto factions of the society. Such conflicts dissipated human energies that might have served more constructive purposes. The failure to uproot color prejudice was due to the fact that it was embedded in the national culture and intertwined with the political and economic structure of the society.

# 3
# Language and Social Mobility

Two languages were spoken in Haiti: Haitian Creole and French. Haitian Creole evolved during the colonial period as a means of communication between the French colonists and the African slaves. French and African languages contributed to its formation.

The early French colonists were chiefly recruited from the lower classes of French society. They were for the most part uneducated and illiterate. They spoke a dialect that probably differed from the standard French of the time. They first came to the Caribbean area as pirates.

While the French colonists may have had a common background, it was not so with the slaves. The latter came from various tribes, and they spoke a variety of languages. The list of the tribes from which the African slaves originated is impressive: Foula, Poulard, Soso, Bambarra, Kiambara, Mandingo, Wolof, Fon, Mahi, Hausa, Ibo, Yoruba, Bini, Takwa, Fida, Amine, Fanti, Agoua, Sobo, Limba, Adja, Salongo, Mayombe, Mousombe, Moundongue, Bumba, Kanga.

Slavery disrupted the natural cultural life of the Africans. Their cultural and linguistic backgrounds were virtually obliterated by the colonial system. Although the majority of the Africans imported to Saint-Domingue came from the Kingdom of Benin, later known as Dahomey, the colonists always separated the people with common ethnic backgrounds so as to reduce the threat of organized slave revolts. This colonial policy hindered the formation of homogenous African linguistic communities and thereby prevented the survival of the African languages.

The management of the slaves required a minimum of verbal communication. One fact was certain: the colonists were not going to learn the languages of their slaves. They could always use the whip. At the most, the French colonists simplified their own language when they addressed the slaves. The latter carried the burden of linguistic assimilation. The simplified, colonial French dialect evolved in time and became what is now known as Creole.[1] It replaced the African languages and became the native tongue of all the blacks in the colony.

A sort of linguistic stratification corresponded to the colonial social structure: French was the language of the civilized human masters; and Creole that of the subhuman slaves, the uncivilized savages. The colonists and the educated freedmen were bilingual, and the others monolingual.

When Haiti became independent in 1804, it adopted French as its official language. The relationship between French and Creole remained the same in post-colonial-Haitian society by virtue of the dominant status accorded to the former. Creole was the native language of all Haitians. The elite was bilingual. It was estimated that less than 10 percent of Haiti's current population—the elite—could read, write, and speak French fluently. Semiliterate Haitians comprised another 3 percent to 5 percent of the total population. The rest of the society was illiterate and strictly monolingual.

The linguistic situation in Haiti was well described by the concept *diglossia,* a term used by Charles A. Ferguson:

> *Diglossia* is a relatively stable-language situation in which, in addition to the primary dialects of the language (which may include a standard or regional standards), there is a very divergent, highly codified (often grammatically more complex) superposed variety, the vehicle of a large and respected body of written literature, either of an earlier period or in another speech community, which is learned largely by formal education and is used for most written and formal spoken purposes but is not used by any sector of the community for ordinary conversation.[2]

Only the Haitian elite was directly affected by *diglossia* for the simple reason that its members alone spoke both French and Creole. The families of the elite tried to expose their children to the French language as much as possible. They discouraged them from using the vernacular. The protection of the elite's children against exposure to Creole was ineffective. They were exposed to it right in their own homes. The maids, who were employed by their families, were Creole speakers and obviously had to be addressed in Creole.

A paradigm will be set up so as to facilitate the analysis of the usage of Creole and French. Two sets of dichotomies will be used: formal vs. informal; and private vs. public activities.

|  | *Private* | *Public* |
|---|---|---|
| *Formal* | French (or Creole) | French |
| *Informal* | Creole | Creole (or French) |

Haitian Creole displaced French in all except formal, public circumstances. Official speeches, radio broadcasts, and conferences were all made in French. French was used almost exclusively in all schools, all governmental and administrative bureaus. French was the only written language. Approximately 80 percent to 90 percent of the population consisted of monolingual Creole speakers who were unable to participate in all social activities requiring a knowledge of French because the two languages were not mutually intelligible. The masses were effectively excluded from the official life of the country. A Haitian could participate fully in the total life of his community only if he was fluent in both the vernacular and the official language.[3]

The author's own experiences in Haiti will help bring an understanding of the linguistic situation to an extent.[4] Ever since he was very young, his parents wanted him to speak French all the time. They spoke French around him as frequently as possible. He also had a baby-sitter who spoke French. But he still learned Creole because it was used often enough around his home. The baby-sitter and the maids would always converse in Creole among themselves, and his parents would address them in Creole as well. Whenever he was taken out, he also heard other people speak Creole. The only way a Haitian could be prevented from learning the native language was by complete isolation from Creole speakers.

The behavior pattern that arose from *diglossia* was somewhat comic. In later years, his mother addressed him in Creole and still expected that he answer her back in French. He often spoke Creole with his brother and sisters and would switch back to French whenever in the presence of parents or relatives. In school, all students had to speak French in class. Once they were dismissed from the classrooms, they spoke Creole among themselves—they spoke Creole in the school yard during recess, on their way home after school, and so on. The students would change to French whenever an instructor approached them. Conversations followed this rule: Creole was spoken among equals (e.g., students), but in the presence of superiors (i.e., educated adults, teachers, parents, and relatives), or when addressing them, French was used.

The use of French was a formality that one sought to cast off as one became older. To do so was a sign of maturity and personal independence. The use of French in conversations with one's parents, one's relatives, and others was, in a way, a sign of submission to their authority; it was an acknowledgment of the higher status or seniority of these people who more or less demanded the use of French. When the children of the elite reached adult status, they were able to use Creole more often and more freely.

The members of the elite usually spoke French in formal–private situations (i.e., receptions, conversations with mere acquaintances), although Creole was also used at times. This happened whenever there was a breakdown in the formality of the situation. The use of Creole then signaled a change in the relation between the interlocutors. The switch from French to Creole could mean a reduction in social distance and greater intimacy. It could also mean that one of the interlocutors became upset; Haitians tend to express themselves in the vernacular whenever they are under an emotional strain. The shift to Creole was also used to express the vulgarity, triviality, or ordinary nature of what was being said; the opposite was true of French. Haitian jokes, especially "dirty" jokes, were told in Creole. In general, the use of Creole between two people of similar status signified that the relationship between them was casual, informal, or intimate (informal–private).

Creole was used in all informal–public situations. Bilingual Haitians might still use French in this situation for purposes of privacy or to call attention to themselves. The use of French in an informal–public context was usually considered pedantic. One fact was clear in Haitian society: prestige, social and economic advantages accrued to people in proportion to their command of French.

It took a greater effort to speak French correctly than Creole. Haitians faced the same uneasiness in writing French: "The conflict between Creole and French manifestly betrays itself in the works of some of our writers. Their style lacks spontaneity and naturalness; it often has the borrowed air of a peasant who put on his Sunday best. In fact, French for them is not the spouting and pure language of thought and sentiment . . ."[5] It was natural that Haitians should feel more comfortable with Creole, which after all was their native tongue.

However, many Haitians were ashamed of Creole. Whenever they were asked what language they spoke, they almost always answered French even though they might have been conversing in Creole, or might not speak French at all. Bilingual Haitians seldom conceded right away that they also spoke Creole, their native tongue. Ferguson remarked that educated Haitians even frequently denied the existence of the vernacular, insisting that they always spoke French.[6]

Haitians generally regarded French as superior to Creole. Where the feeling of superiority of French was not so strong, there was still a belief that it was somehow more beautiful, more logical, better able to express important thoughts, and the like.[7]

In the Haitian social milieu, one's ability to express oneself in French was perceived as an added value to one's being, a means of social advancement, a pass to go to certain places, or a permit to sit in certain living rooms.[8]

Bellegarde, as a member of the elite, well expressed how some Haitians felt when they spoke French.

> The usage of a common language has naturally created deep mental affinities between Haitian people and French people. Two peoples who use the same words to express the same joys and the same pains, who translate by the same vocables their efforts for the conquest of happiness and knowledge, cannot remain strangers to one another: their souls communicate by means of invisible channels which carry sentiments and thoughts from one to the other, and it is not surprising that the same ideal of life and beauty gradually imposes itself in their mind.[9]

Bellegarde felt that the Haitians who possessed a good command of French had a consciousness similar to that of French people. Frantz Fanon, a renowned psychoanalyst, concurred with this view: "A man who has a language consequently possesses the world expressed and implied by that language."[10] France was the main center of cultural inspiration for the Haitian elite (although the United States was exercising some cultural influences on the country too).[11] Its members thought that they could equal the French in status through the assimilation of the French language and culture.

> Every colonized people—in other words, every people in whose soul an inferiority complex has been created by the death and burial of its local cultural originality—finds itself face to face with the language of the civilizing nation; that is, with the culture of the mother country. The colonized is elevated above his jungle status in proportion to his adoption of the mother country's cultural standards. He becomes whiter as he renounces his blackness, his jungle.[12]

From this illusion arose the self-hatred and complex of inferiority that afflicted Haitians. No degree of cultural assimilation was going to earn them equality with the French who were largely absent from their social environment. In addition, they were themselves victim of the French's ethnocentrism, which they had adopted in their acculturation.

The root of the problem was this: the black man was not a man in the white world where he lived.[13] Consequently, he felt that he had to be white in order to be human.[14] He wanted to prove at all costs the richness of his thought and the equal value of his intellect.[15] Creole reminded the elite of its racial and cultural inferiority from the perspective of the white world. Its contempt for Creole was its way of coping with this inferiority complex. French, on the other hand, provided and preserved the high status which it enjoyed in Haitian society.

Since Creole and French were not mutually intelligible, the communications barrier between Creole speakers and French speakers constituted a linguistic cleavage that separated the elite from the masses and prevented the development of democratic institutions. Imagine the illiterate Haitian masses being stirred by an official political speech in French. This situation actually promoted political apathy. The masses had little involvement in the politics of the country. The maintenance of French as the official language since independence merely helped preserve the privileges of the educated elite.

Haitian leaders long considered education an important factor in national development. Ignorance and illiteracy obstructed all other forms of progress. However, French, as the main vehicle of instruction in the schools, hindered rather than facilitated the propagation of education to the illiterate masses. That is because the mode of acquisition of the official language and the vernacular differed. The former was taught formally in schools with the help of grammars, dictionaries, treatises on pronunciation, style, and so forth. Its orthography was standardized, and the established norm for pronunciation, grammar, and vocabulary allowed little variation. On the other hand, the vernacular was learned naturally during the normal process of socialization. Its grammar was learned without any explicit discussion of grammatical concepts, while its pronunciation and vocabulary varied widely.[16]

Other impediments to educational progress doubtlessly existed. The best and the majority of the schools were located in the urban centers, whereas 80 percent to 90 percent of the population lived in the rural areas. Besides, although education was compulsory through primary school, there lacked enough schools to accommodate the whole school-age population. Only 24 percent of school-age youth attended school, and the majority of this percentage was made up of students from the elite. The student dropout rate was also very high, particularly in primary school. The country had the highest illiteracy rate in the American hemisphere.

Creole offered a better and more efficient means of eradicating illiteracy. Since the Haitian masses already spoke the language, they could easily receive instructions in it. It sufficed then to provide them with the ability to write and read it. French was, on the contrary, foreign to the masses. A literacy program in French meant that they had to be taught a whole new language before they could receive any instructions at all. Creole was for these reasons a far better choice for the promotion of national development.

This position was supported by J. P. Morose in his analysis of the Haitian educational system. According to him, Creole was the sole linguistic tool that would allow the nation to pull itself out of ignorance by the rapid diffusion of an efficacious, functional literacy program.[17] The UNESCO committee on education also concurred with this after the conclusion of its study on illiteracy around the world. Its recommendation was that a pupil should begin his formal educaton in his native language and should continue to be taught in that language as long as the supply of books and materials permit.[18] To reject Creole as a teaching language at the level of basic education would simply maintain the status quo and help perpetuate ignorance and underdevelopment in Haiti.[19]

Language was, indeed, an important issue where national

development was concerned. It played a predominant role in the cultural orientation of people.[20] It facilitated the assumption of a culture.[21] Educated Haitians supported French culture, unfortunately at the expense of their own. Their French orientation alienated them from the rest of the society. They were too busy trying to be French to pay any serious attention to the local national problems. The conditions of *diglossia* obstructed social, political, and economic progress.

The choice of a language for national development would certainly have to be based on more than an ideological basis. So, a careful analysis of the pros and cons of each language was critical.

French had its advantages as the official language of Haiti. It was an international language with prestige. The French-speaking Haitian community was linked linguistically to the other French-speaking communities of the world. The most important asset of the French language was its respected and large body of accumulated literature in the various fields of knowledge.

However, these benefits were only enjoyed by a very small percentage of the Haitian population. The argument that French, as an already well-established language, was better suited for national development was often made by the members of the elite. If French had not helped Haiti for over the century and a half that it was its official language, it was not about to do so any time soon in the future.

Haitian Creole did have its disadvantages. It was a relatively new language with no substantial body of literature, spoken only as the vernacular of a few island peoples. Such obstacles could be overcome nonetheless: "Whatever considerations may affect the choice of a language for science or administration in a newly independent nation, this at least can be made clear: all languages are equally capable of being developed for all purposes, and no language is any less qualified to be the vehicle of modern science and technology than were English and Russian some centuries ago."[22]

No doubt a great deal of prejudice would have to be overcome aside from the real disadvantages of Creole. "They [Creoles] are languages in the defined sense of the word; some of them are already used as literary media, and they would be fully viable as media of education and science. At present they tend to be more discriminated against than languages with a more conventional history. But there is no justification for discriminating against any language whatever."²³ The proposal that Creole be recognized as the official language of Haiti was made a number of times and was met with strong resistance from the elite and the government.

What policy should be followed in the choice of Haiti's official language?

1. *National development*:   History showed that French did not contribute to national development in any meaningful way for over 175 years (of course, all the blame did not rest on the French language alone). Creole seemed to offer a more promising future with the advantages that it would afford in a literacy campaign and the spread of education to the masses.

2. *Democratization*:   Creole would evidently be the language of democracy in Haiti since 80 percent to 90 percent of the population consisted of monolingual Creole speakers.

3. *Unity*:   The population as a whole was unified linguistically through Creole, whereas French divided the society.

4. *Foreign relations*:   What was most feared by the elite was the linguistic and cultural isolation of the country were Haitian Creole to become the official language. Pro-French Haitians had urged instead the teaching of French to the masses so as to "civilize" them and break their isolation from the rest of the world.

The question was whether Haiti could afford the money and the time to set up and implement such a literacy program. The answer was no. The country would also have to pay a heavy psychocultural price for the "Frenchification" of its whole population; would not the alienation of the society be further promoted by it?

On the other hand, people assert that French is a necessity for the Haitian peasant on the international plane. This argument could carry a certain weight in the long run. But in the short run, it manifestly lacks realism. Besides, to know how to read and write in Creole in no way impedes the eventual ulterior learning of French. This is on the contrary the best method and the surest means to learn French, the language most closely related to Haitian Creole, about 80 percent of the vocabulary of which is constituted of vocables used in French. Thus, it is wrong to believe that literacy in Creole would isolate the Haitian. One fact can be lived or verified by any Haitian. It is that illiteracy, maintained especially on account of the dispensation of education in French, prevents all exchange of personal correspondence between parents, sons, friends, acquaintances who live in different cities within the country itself. When a father who wants to write to his son, or when a young man who wishes to write to his fiancée has to resort to the good offices of a scribe so that the latter translate into French what has been dictated to him in Creole, the scene, however picturesque it may be, is not any less alienating for the illiterate. There is the first isolation—the one that reigns inside the country among the illiterate 90 percent of the population—that a literacy program in Creole could break.[24]

Creole evidently offered certain advantages worth considering, advantages which would benefit the society as a whole. Creole should have shared the official status of French in Haiti. After years of debate, this finally happened in 1974 under the government of Jean-Claude Duvalier, and in 1979 it was formally introduced in the schools as a teaching language. It will be some time before anyone will be able to assess the impact of this new policy. Much will depend upon how it is implemented.

# 4

# The Foreign Influences

The word neocolonialism has been used quite frequently by leaders of the developing countries,[1] social scientists, and writers dealing with the Third World.[2] It referred to the survival of the colonial system in spite of formal recognition of political independence in emerging countries that became the victims of an indirect and subtle form of domination by political, economic, social, military, or technical means.[3] Haiti was a perfect example of it.

Haiti officially proclaimed its independence from France on January 1, 1804 amidst social and economic chaos. The economy of the former colony had been ruined by the wars of independence. In addition, the new nation also faced the hostility of the colonial powers. Haiti was then surrounded by slave-owning colonies. The United States, the only other independent country in the Americas in 1804, also had a slave economy. The slave-owning world refused to recognize Haiti's independence for fear that it would jeopardize its economic system. France and Spain called for an international trade embargo in an effort to strangle the Haitian revolution economically. The country remained in virtual isolation during the first two decades of its independence, all the while fearing another French invasion.

Internal social conditions were alarming. The freedmen and the slaves of Saint-Domingue had been united only by the need to overthrow their common oppressor. Now that they were faced with the arduous task of nation building, rather than continue

their cooperative partnership, they became, instead, two antagonistic social classes.

The first order of business on the morrow of independence
was the redistribution of wealth. The newly freed slaves constituted the majority of the population, and they owned nothing.
Conflicts arising from this issue set apart the former freedmen
and the newly freed blacks within the government itself and
resulted in the assassination of Dessalines, the first head of state
and chief founder of Haiti.

The former freedmen were reactionary. They were primarily
interested in the improvement of their own position in the society.
They were otherwise ready to cooperate with the imperialist
powers. The existence of potential or de facto Haitian collabo-
rators was an important factor in the establishment of neocolonialism. This form of indirect colonial rule required the
collaboration of a segment of the society. One can easily see why
the former freedmen would play this role once their position in
colonial times is understood. In Saint-Domingue, the freedmen
could own property, including slaves. Some of them had even
been educated in France, and a great many of them had been
fathered by the French colonists. They had been among the
most thoroughly assimilated elements of colonial society. They
wanted equality with the white colonists. Only when they failed
to obtain it by their own efforts did they join forces with the
slaves against the colonists.

Besides, the colonial system hardly prepared the freedmen
and the slaves for the eventuality of independence. There was
little in the colonial past that could help them in nation building.
Saint-Domingue had been little more than a vast forced labor
camp. The government of Toussaint Louverture was the only
instance where some blacks had exercised any kind of administrative duties. Toussaint was himself an exceptional man by
ability, education, and achievement. Unfortunately, his administration did not last long. He tried to dismantle the racist structure of the colony and also attempted to establish a locally
autonomous government, one that was more responsive to the
needs of the colony instead of those of the metropolis. Never-

theless, he was ready to collaborate with the French despite the relative autonomy of his government. The form of government that he sought to establish was similar to the protectorates or dependencies that were organized later on by the colonial powers. He was much too far ahead of his time in the eighteenth century. Napoleon rejected his ideas and sent French troops to reestablish direct colonial rule over Saint-Domingue.

In 1804, the Haitian nation was a loose aggregate of people who had newly won political autonomy but had none of the tools necessary to build an independent society practically from scratch. Haitian leaders, aside from their greater expertise in the military, held little advantage over the ignorant masses. Dessalines, the first chief of state, was an illiterate former slave. He was an extraordinary military commander but a poor political leader and administrator.

The former freedmen saw themselves as the natural inheritors of the French colonists' social and political status after independence. As the attempts to continue the operation of the large, colonial plantations failed, the new elite had to settle for the intermediary sector of the economy, namely commerce, and the government that had become an important source of its income. Access to political power meant access to wealth and prestige. Every single Haitian head of state, with very few exceptions, tried to remain in power as long as possible—not so much for the good of the country as for the plunder of the public treasury. As a result, a great measure of insecurity and instability continuously affected the society. Of the twenty-six heads of state who succeeded each other between January 1804 and July 1915, when the American marines landed, fifteen were ousted by force and sent into exile, four were assassinated, four died in office, two retired to private life, and one committed suicide. The country's economy was drained by these incessant insurrections and the excesses of those in power.

Haiti was very vulnerable to foreign influence under these conditions. The French were allowed back in the country as educators, technical experts, and commercial agents. A significant number of other foreigners came as well: Syrians, Germans,

Italians, and Americans among others. They all became involved in the commercial sector. They monopolized the import–export trade and penetrated the market of wholesale and retail trade, sweeping aside the Haitian businessmen who could not survive their competition. Many of these foreigners also involved themselves in local Haitian politics.

The Syrians, fleeing Turkish persecutions, began to arrive in Haiti in the 1900s. They invaded the commercial sector, from import–export trade all the way down to retail trade. Many of them crisscrossed the country as peddlers and went into the remotest towns, where they put local merchants out of business. They caused so much resentment in the small trade sector that the government was forced to take measures to protect the local Haitian businessmen from foreign competition.

The Germans occupied an important position in the economy at the turn of the century. They owned most of the public utilities, and German shipping companies handled the bulk of Haitian trade. Their influence considerably declined following the war of 1914 to 1918.

The Italians were mostly involved in the shoemaking industry and the jewelry business.[4]

The French exercised the greatest influence prior to the American Occupation. They owned and operated the first and only national bank from 1881 to 1910. The bank was founded with French capital and French technical assistance, and it operated under French management by agreement with the Haitian government. It collected the principal revenues of the country, acted as depository for official funds and the national paymaster, and monitored the interests of foreign creditors.[5] After scandalous frauds involving the French directors and some Haitian employees, the bank was reorganized and became owned collectively by French, American, and German interests in 1910.

While Haiti doubtlessly needed international aid, the help that was provided almost always involved conflicts of interest. The various foreign powers competed for exclusive influence over the country. In this climate, Haiti's national interests were often sacrificed to serve those of the imperialist powers. Internal social conditions also made it difficult for the country to take full advantage of the aid that it received.

The international community was rather inhospitable since independence. The country was a small fish in a sea of sharks. Its leaders constantly feared the loss of its precarious sovereignty. They were often forced to yield to the demands of the foreign powers. This will be illustrated through a discussion of Haiti's relations with three countries: France, Germany, and the United States.


## FRANCE

The nation was maintained in a continuous state of alert during its first years of independence on account of France's refusal to recognize Haiti's political autonomy. To prepare against the threat of a French invasion, Dessalines and his generals undertook the fortification of the country and gave a militaristic organization to the society.

Rather than invade, France tried to negotiate the restoration of its rule. In 1814, Louis XVIII sent a delegation to Haiti to persuade President Pétion to accept the hegemony of France. Pétion refused. King Henry I (Christophe)[6] was then approached by the French envoy on the same matter. The latter put the envoy to death. Another French commission was sent again in 1816, and it once more failed to accomplish its mission.

President Boyer (1818-1843) was obsessed by the danger of a French attack on the country. Haiti had no allies. No country had yet recognized its independence. Consequently, he decided to negotiate with France. The first attempts proved fruitless.

A parley in Brussels in 1823 also proved sterile, and in 1824, after further French entreaties, Haitian agents offered an indemnity to the former colonists in exchange for recognition of Haitian sovereignty. Charles X still thought, however, that France should retain ultimate sovereignty while devolving local autonomy to Haitians. In 1825, he peremptorily brought the tortuous negotiations to an end by issuing an ordinance which, while patronizingly recognizing the independence of

Haiti, demanded preferential tariff arrangements for goods to and from France and required Haiti to pay 150 million francs in five annual installments. Three squadrons . . . of the French fleet accompanied the presentation of the ordinance to Boyer in Port-au-Prince; the use of gunboat diplomacy thus made it difficult for the Haitians to refuse to accept such a heavy indemnity.[7]

The decaying economy resulting from the collapse of the large plantations could not bear the burden of this outrageous debt. Boyer only managed to pay the first annual installment. France reviewed the situation in 1838 and decided to recognize Haitian independence unconditionally and simultaneously reduced the amount of the indemnity to 60 million francs payable over thirty years.

In 1825, France was the first nation to recognize Haiti's independence. Other European nations followed thereafter. The United States traded with Haiti but refused to grant diplomatic recognition until 1862, under the administration of Abraham Lincoln.

## GERMANY

The Germans constituted a stable and influential colony of about 200 around 1909 to 1910. As the Haitian government sought to protect Haitian business interests by giving Haitian citizens preferential treatment, they took up Haitian citizenship and even married Haitian women. Approximately 80 percent of all exports of coffee and imports of consumer goods and textiles were controlled by them. They also owned the public utilities in Port-au-Prince, the capital city, and Cap-Haitien.

They were very much implicated in the political upheavals of Haiti: "Influential Germans made fortunes by underwriting revolutions—double their money back if their side won—which was usually the case, until the next revolution, for the poorly paid government army . . . rarely put up much of a fight."[8] They also interfered with local affairs in other ways. The Luders Affair stands as another example of gunboat diplomacy.

Luders, a German citizen, was arrested by Haitian authorities for interfering with the arrest of a Haitian citizen. He was charged with assault and battery on a police officer. A Haitian court found him guilty and sentenced him to jail and the payment of a fine. Luders protested his conviction and appealed to the German government for help. Foreign diplomatic pressures urged the Haitian government to work out a settlement so as to avoid German intervention in the dispute. Luders was tried again and found guilty for a second time. As this solution failed to appease the diplomatic community, the government pardoned Luders on October 22, 1897. Luders left the country immediately. On December 6, 1897, two German warships came into the bay of Port-au-Prince to present an ultimatum to the Haitian government. Commander Thiele demanded an indemnity of twenty thousand dollars for Luders and the assurance that he would be allowed back in the country, a written apology to the German government, a twenty-one gun salute to the German flag, and the acceptance of these demands within four hours. The defenseless Haitian government capitulated and suffered the humiliation.

## THE UNITED STATES

The American marines landed in Haiti in July 1915. Factors in both countries led to this intervention. The islands of the Caribbean held a strategic place in the American military defense system. (Before their occupation, Americans had been interested in the Môle-Saint Nicholas as a possible site for a naval coaling station. In addition to being an excellent natural port, the Windward Passage and the Panama Canal could easily be controlled from there.) The United States assigned to itself the role of policeman for the Americas and adopted the policy of preventing foreign intervention in the hemisphere. The American intervention in Haiti was then rendered necessary by the political and economic chaos that invited direct interference by the European powers involved.

The following events preceded the American Occupation. As the country's finances were continuously mismanaged amidst political instability and administrative corruption, the National Bank, owned then by the French, proposed to the Haitian government that it be allowed to administer Haitian customs in 1899. Its request was turned down as the government was reluctant to give up control over its principal source of revenue. The bank made the same request in 1909 and failed again to win the assent of the government. After the reorganization in 1910, the French, German, and American interest groups in the bank would all lay claim to the control of Haitian customs.

In 1910, the Haitian government negotiated a loan with France. When the American government learned of this, it intervened diplomatically and sought to impose its participation in the financial deal. The American intent was to reduce the threat of French intervention in Haiti. The Haitian government allayed American fears by signing the MacDonald Contract with an American entrepreneur (1910). James P. MacDonald, an American citizen, was to build a railroad from Port-au-Prince to Cap-Haitien, and on the nonoccupied lands of the National Domain within twenty kilometers on both sides of the railroad, all along the line, he was to establish banana plantations. The land was leased to him at the nominal rent of one dollar per acre for a period of fifty years. The government had to pay for the railroad.

Haiti stopped paying MacDonald in 1914 because it was dissatisfied with the construction of the line. A litigation ensued between the two parties. The American government intervened on MacDonald's behalf and started pressuring the Haitian government to continue the payments for the unfinished railroad line.

The increased American involvement in Haitian affairs in 1914 led to a brief military intervention that year: In November 1914, President Zamor was ousted by Theodore, who inherited the financial mess. He tried to forcibly remove from the bank state funds (part of the 1910 loan) placed there to redeem paper currency. Because this was a violation of the terms of the loan, and because the bank had already asked the United States for financial control of Haitian customs, the bank then called for United States' protection.[9] American marines landed in Port-au-Prince on December 17, 1914. They went directly to the National Bank where they seized the state funds ($500,000 in gold). They returned to their ship with the gold and took it to the United States, where they deposited it in a New York bank at an interest rate of 2 percent. The whole operation was carried out without the least resistance.

Conditions worsened within a few months, and the marines came back in July 1915. This time they stayed until 1934. The Americans took over the whole government, except the Department of Education and the post office.

The occupation naturally facilitated the infusion of American capital in the country. Before July 1915, American interests in Haiti included the wharf of Port-au-Prince, the national electric company, the railway company, the National Railroad, and a 40-percent share in the National Bank. The occupation opened the floodgates to such a swarm of new American companies that it is impossible to give an exact listing of them. The United States tried to shore up the economy by reviving large-scale agriculture. This was made possible by an amendment to the Haitian Constitution allowing foreign ownership of land for the first time since its independence. The following is a partial list of the American interests that invaded the agricultural sector:[10]

> Haytian American Sugar Company (1915): 24,000 acres.
> Haytian Products Company (1915): 10,000 acres.
> United West Indies Corporation (1918): 16,000 acres.
> Société Commerciale d'Haïti (1918): 3,000 acres.
> North Haytian Sugar Company (1922): 400 acres.
> Haytian Pine-apple Company (1923): 600 acres.
> Haytian American Development Corporation (1926): 14,000 acres.
> Haytian Agricultural Corporation (1927): 2,200 acres.

From the ten companies that tried their luck between 1915 and 1930, only two survived and prospered.[11] By 1934, the

Standard Fruit Company could be added to the list of American investors in Haiti.

Haiti not only fell prey to neocolonialism but also lost its independence entirely during the occupation. Foreign economic influences and the irresponsible leadership of the elite created conditions that eroded the country's political autonomy. An analysis of Haiti's foreign debt prior to the American Occupation will provide further insight into the causes of foreign intervention.

Haiti's foreign debts started in 1825 with the indemnity of 150 million francs owed to France in exchange for the recognition of its independence. President Boyer borrowed 30 million francs from Lafitte Company, a French firm, and completed the net sum of the loan (24 million francs) with funds from the nearly bankrupt treasury to pay the first installment of 30 million francs to France. Subsequently, neither the remaining installments of the National Independence Debt nor the terms of the private French loan could be met by the impoverished government. When France reduced the indemnity to 60 million francs in 1838, Haiti then owed a total of 90 million francs. The payment of this debt was completed in 1887.

Two other loans were contracted in the 1870s: the first, 3 million piastres in 1874; and the second, 12 million piastres in 1875 included the right of redemption of the first loan. The Crédit Général Français, which made the loan, deducted a commission in the amount of 9,517,234.50 piastres![12]

The government of T. S. Sam (March 1896-May 1902) came in the wake of political and financial chaos. The country had been torn by a civil war and numerous insurrections from 1888 to 1896. The national economy was in deplorable conditions. He borrowed, in all, over 37 million francs by the beginning of his term. When he left in 1902, Haiti was still in a financial mess.

The government of F. A. Simon borrowed another 75 million francs in 1910 from L'Union Parisienne. This loan was earmarked for the payment of the previous debts contracted in 1875 and 1896—and for the establishment of the National Bank.

France was the source of all these loans. The Haitian foreign debt amounted to over 100 million francs in February 1914:[13]

| Year loans contracted: | Principal Amount in French francs: | Year of maturity: |
|---|---|---|
| 1875 | 10,799,580 | 1922 |
| 1896 | 37,988,500 | 1932 |
| 1910 | 64,368,500 | 1961 |
| Total | 113,156,580 | |

The question is: Where did all this money go? A big chunk of it was consumed by the governments that had to put down numerous revolts. Some of the loaned money was used to finance the governments' politico-bureaucratic machines. Another portion served to reduce inflation. The rest doubtlessly found its way into the pockets of corrupt Haitian politicians.

By 1914, the intermediary sector of the Haitian economy, including the National Bank, was completely dominated by foreigners. The political instability jeopardized their economic interests and incited the intervention of the foreign powers.

The years from 1934 to the present saw a repeat of the previous historical pattern without much improvement in the fiscal and political administration of the country. The international environment has changed since World War II with the rise of communism and, particularly, the Cuban Revolution. Haiti's geographic proximity to communist Cuba turned it into a potential battleground for rival world powers. This international political situation served to further jeopardize the country's relative independence.

The involvement of Haiti in the larger ideological struggle between the capitalist and communist world invited further interference in its internal affairs by the implicated foreign powers. The national leaders exploited this international ideological conflict to obtain foreign aid and keep afloat the bankrupt government. Despite the best intentions, much of this foreign aid was wasted by the inefficient and corrupt political bureaucracy. The result was the perpetuation of a corrupt and authoritarian political system that fostered little economic growth.

# 5

# What Happened to the Haitian Economy

The foundations of Haiti's economy were laid during the colonial period. Saint-Domingue was France's most prosperous colony in the eighteenth century. The colonists amassed considerable fortunes in the sugar industry. The prosperity of the colonial sugar plantations rested on the legions of African slaves who made up 87 percent of the total population.

The French colonial population was transitory in nature. The colonists seldom intended to settle in Saint-Domingue and make it their new home. It was a place where they came to enrich themselves as quickly as they could and then return to the mother country. Absentee ownership of the colonial estates was very common.

The colonial economy was an appendage of that of the metropolis. Saint-Domingue primarily produced for France under a trade monopoly. Under this arrangement, the colony could only trade with France, using French ships and subject to French colonial regulations. The colony exported raw materials and agricultural crops while it imported manufactured goods and foodstuffs from the metropolis. This colonial scheme was designed to increase the wealth of the mother country.

These conditions were unfavorable to the planters of Saint-Domingue. They would have liked to do business with those parties that would have secured them the highest profits. They suffered other disadvantages as well. Metropolitan loans to the planters carried maximum interest rates, and the price of the colony's exports was largely determined by the metropolitan markets that also set the price of the metropolitan products to to be exchanged with the colonists. The planters possessed little bargaining power; they were at the mercy of the metropolis.

The attractive opportunities available outside of the French economic sphere led the French colonists to circumvent the economic constraints placed upon them by France. Trade went on with other countries in defiance of the colonial administration. Smuggling and black markets could not be suppressed totally on account of the difficulties involved in the enforcement of the colonial regulations.

The model of economic relationship between France and Saint-Domingue could be viewed as a chain of exploitation: the slaves were exploited by the freedmen and the colonists who were in turn exploited by the bankers and merchants of the metropolis. The colonial charter that regulated trade with Saint-Domingue operated in favor of the metropolitan bankers and merchants at the expense of the colonists. The latter were interested in obtaining higher profits for themselves. This conflict of interest represented the major source of discontent between the planters of Saint-Domingue and the metropolis. The planters began to agitate for greater local autonomy while the Revolution of 1789 was taking place in France.

The French Revolution of 1789 inspired the *affranchis*,[1] who also agitated for political rights in Saint-Domingue. The latent antagonism between the slaves and their masters led to a major slave revolt during the same period. The colonial armies and administration were then confronted by all three sectors of the colony up in arms. In addition, Saint-Domingue was also under attack by the English and the Spaniards from the west and the east respectively. Saint-Domingue was disintegrating politically and economically in this chaotic situation. Toussaint Louverture emerged as the only leader capable of creating order out of this mess. He reestablished peace in the French colony and even won the rest of the island for France. He gave local autonomy to the colony and made himself the governor of the whole island.

By the start of the nineteenth century, the new political developments in Saint-Domingue were as follows: a former black slave was ruling the colony; there were high-ranking black officers in the colonial army; slavery had been abolished; and the colony was locally autonomous with a constitution ratified in 1801. The slaves had been freed out of necessity since 1793, but they were still bound to the plantations.

Except for the change in the legal status of the blacks, nothing had been altered in the colonial economic sector. The plantations were reactivated under Toussaint with new labor regulations. Toussaint divided the island into a number of districts that were administered by generals from the colonial army. The generals served as the military commanders, administrators, and plantation inspectors of their districts. Work on the plantations was organized severely. The freed slaves, excluding those who were in the colonial army, had to stay on the plantations where they previously had been enslaved. They had to work on them for a period of three to five years, and they were to receive a third of the plantations' crops in compensation for their labor. The laborers were closely supervised by the army. Heavy penalties were administered to the plantation workers on counts of vagrancy and idleness.

France did not accept Toussaint's politico-economic deal. Metropolitan armies were sent to suppress his government. Saint-Domingue was plunged once more into revolutionary turmoil, leading to the independence of Haiti in 1804. The plantations and the whole economy of the territory were devastated. The French colonists were expelled.

The colonial world viewed Haiti as a threat and, consequently, isolated it diplomatically and economically. Spain and France stopped trading with Haiti and continuously urged the other European nations and the United States to do the same. The United States and England were among the few nations that still traded with Haiti. Trade was vital to the country, especially at that time. The new nation did not even produce enough food to feed its population.

The changes that were brought on by the Revolution of 1803

affected the superstructure of the society rather than its infra-structure. The economy remained essentially unchanged.

Dessalines had been one of Toussaint's lieutenants. As head of the new state in 1804, he was unable to give new economic organization to the society. He knew no other economic model but that of the colony and Toussaint's version of it. He adopted the latter. The former slaves could be either soldiers or culti-vators, whereas the former freedmen became plantation owners (which most of them already were), civil servants, military offi-cers, professionals, or businessmen. The cultivators were assigned work on the plantations under military supervision for a stipu-lated period of time. They received a portion of the harvests in payment, as under Toussaint's regulations.

The immediate successors of Dessalines offered two alterna-tive economic systems to the country. There was Christophe's model in the north, and Pétion's in the south: a kingdom and a republic respectively. Christophe established a feudal system in Toussaint's tradition. He created a nobility, something that Des-salines had refused to do. He rented the large plantations to his nobles, whom he held responsible for their administration and for the management of the laborers who were attached to the land as serfs. The economy was strictly regulated by the king-dom, namely the absolute monarch himself. Pétion's government advocated the doctrine of laissez-faire. Pétion interfered the least with the economy of the Republic, except insofar as gov-ernment land grants and property taxes were concerned. Pétion's model survived in Haiti despite the fact that it had not been successful. The Republic was bankrupt at the end of Pétion's administration, whereas Christophe left at his death a treasury with substantial reserves. What counted most against Christophe's model was the harshness of his regime and the almost inhumane discipline that he had imposed upon his subjects and nobles.

After the abolition of slavery, discipline and legalized coercion were about the only means to insure a labor supply for the plantations. The newly freed slaves, men and women, had neither economic incentives nor any other strong motivation that would have led them to sell their labor to the plantation owners. No man wanted to exchange his labor for subsistence wages when he could provide for his own subsistence. Although most of the fertile lowlands were taken up by the plantations, there was plenty of marginal land in the mountains. Upon the relaxation of labor regulations, the people went about settling on the vacant lands of the public domain, carving out small subsistence farms.

The country went into an economic crisis as the large plantations deteriorated. The production of sugarcane declined as a result of this. Since sugar represented the country's major source of revenue on the foreign markets, the national economy suffered terribly. The implications were grave for the nation, especially when it was not economically self-sufficient but depended heavily on external trade. Servile labor had constituted the basis of colonial prosperity. The system of large plantations and lowland crops collapsed when it became deprived of its supply of cheap labor.

Small family farms became preponderant in the Haitian economy. The small farms were located mostly in the mountainous areas; there were few squatter settlements on the large plantations of the plains. Coffee gradually replaced sugarcane as the main export crop of Haiti. Coffee was well suited for cultivation in the mountains, and Haitian farmers grew it for export to supplement their subsistence farming. The rise of Haiti's peasantry can be traced back to this transition from the system of large plantations to the emergence of small property owners in the countryside, and to the switch from sugar to coffee as the principal export crop. The large plantations were definitely extinct in Haiti by the second half of the nineteenth century. They were not revived until the American Occupation.

The economy maintained its colonial nature up to the present in that it was still geared toward the production of agricultural crops for foreign markets in exchange for foreign manufactured goods. The infrastructure of the country reflected this orientation. Local markets and transportation continued to center in the port towns, with tenuous roads into the interior to bring out the products for exportation.[2]

The sphere of commercial activities was the key sector of the economy, not only because the country was not self-sufficient but also because it was a major source of revenue for the government. This was the reason why various Haitian leaders wanted to keep the large plantations in operation.

The revenues of the Haitian government came from two principal sources: a) internal taxes, and b) taxes levied by customs on imports and exports. The revenues of the government were obtained from the following sources for the budget of fiscal 1934.[3]

| | | | | |
|---|---|---|---:|---:|
| Customs: | 1. | Importations | $3,878,847.16 | 52.75% |
| | 2. | Exportations | 2,177,747.41 | 29.60% |
| | 3. | Others | 30,041.98 | 0.41% |
| Internal Taxes | | | 1,009,780.41 | 13.75% |
| Other Revenues of the Government | | | 199,846.56 | 2.72% |
| Deductions from Commune Revenues | | | 54,169.53 | 0.74% |
| | | Total | $7,350,433.05 | 100% |

It was clear that the Haitian government derived over 80 percent of its revenues from customs duties that year. Today, customs duties still constitute a significant percentage of the government's revenues; however, the bankrupt government is now heavily subsidized by foreign economic aid. The importance of Haitian customs was further emphasized by the fact that when the country could not pay its debts prior to the occupation, the foreign powers wanted very much to seize control of this source of revenue.

Since the American Occupation, Haiti traded chiefly with the United States. Over half of its foreign trade was with the United States. Haitian exportations generally included products like coffee, cocoa, bananas, and sisal. Importations from the United States consisted of cement, fish, flour, cars, trucks, tires and air tubes, cotton and textile, machines and tools, leather, soap, tobacco, paper, silk, perfume, and chemical products.[4] Haiti's foreign trade followed the colonial pattern, as can be seen by the type of goods exchanged. Haiti was unable to control the price of its exports on the foreign markets, and neither could it determine the price of the foreign goods that it imported. This sort of trade perpetuated the economic dependency and under-development of the country.

The involvement of a great portion of the country's land in the production of export crops caused the neglect of internal domestic needs. The country was unable to produce enough food for its population, which meant that foodstuffs had to be imported. This was one aspect of the country's dependency on foreign markets. On the other hand, the export crops grown in Haiti were also cultivated elsewhere, in most cases, in greater quantity so that the country was in a poor position to compete on the foreign markets. The only way that Haiti was able to overcome, in part, the tough competition on the foreign markets was by making trade agreements with certain nations, giving them special advantages.

Another factor that worked to the detriment of the Haitian economy was the imbalance of trade that existed between Haiti and several other nations, among them France, the United States, England, and Canada. Here are some figures concerning Haiti's commerce with the United States since the beginning of the twentieth century and up to the Haitian fiscal year of 1951 to 1952:[5]

## HAITIAN–AMERICAN TRADE

| Years | | Importations from the US | | Exportations to the US |
|-------|-------|--------------------------|-------|------------------------|
| 1900-01 | Total | $ 3,523,612 | Total | $ 1,363,930 |
| 1901-02 | | 3,034,310 | | 1,662,207 |
| 1902-03 | | 2,611,305 | | 1,297,480 |
| 1903-04 | | 3,551,233 | | 1,500,724 |
| 1904-05 | | 2,535,695 | | 1,214,653 |
| 1905-06 | | 3,594,240 | | 1,412,731 |
| 1906-07 | | 3,153,069 | | 1,500,085 |
| 1907-08 | | 4,004,852 | | 1,010,522 |
| 1908-09 | | 4,114,024 | | 699,123 |
| 1909-10 | | 5,265,056 | | 1,169,355 |

| Years | Importations from the US | Exportations to the US |
|---|---|---|
| 1910-11 | 6,648,675 | 857,263 |
| 1911-12 | 7,761,789 | 824,541 |
| 1912-13 | 6,827,765 | 944,753 |
| 1913-14 | 6,794,925 | 785,292 |
| 1914-15 | 3,395,638 | 1,840,007 |
| 1915-16 | 6,288,016 | 2,560,340 |
| 1916-17 | 7,478,228 | 3,926,953 |
| 1917-18 | 9,423,346 | 5,085,716 |
| 1918-19 | 15,939,529 | 9,546,056 |
| 1919-20 | 22,773,762 | 9,903,881 |
| 1920-21 | 9,543,011 | 1,603,652 |
| 1921-22 | 10,359,613 | 1,438,755 |
| 1922-23 | 11,524,566 | 1,976,572 |
| 1923-24 | 11,817,336 | 1,329,251 |
| 1924-25 | 15,567,869 | 2,318,619 |
| 1925-26 | 14,030,158 | 1,377,767 |
| 1927-28 | 15,246,508 | 1,853,320 |
| 1928-29 | 12,041,145 | 1,306,361 |
| 1929-30 | 9,000,767 | 1,304,657 |
| 1930-31 | 6,577,594 | 727,226 |
| 1931-32 | 5,042,456 | 585,154 |
| 1932-33 | 4,770,187 | 583,818 |
| 1933-34 | 4,421,427 | 905,528 |
| 1934-35 | 3,982,847 | 859,936 |
| 1935-36 | 4,283,218 | 1,345,489 |
| 1936-37 | 4,698,380 | 2,500,351 |
| 1937-38 | 4,125,525 | 2,972,123 |
| 1938-39 | 5,092,802 | 2,502,206 |
| 1939-40 | 5,767,291 | 2,787,437 |
| 1940-41 | 6,177,222 | 5,842,873 |
| 1941-42 | 6,444,691 | 6,813,779 |
| 1942-43 | 7,551,234 | 8,540,715 |
| 1943-44 | 11,324,710 | 10,485,103 |
| 1944-45 | 10,737,678 | 13,302,541 |
| 1945-46 | 13,687,539 | 12,138,639 |
| 1946-47 | 23,915,123 | 18,785,591 |
| 1947-48 | 26,299,258 | 18,491,755 |
| 1948-49 | 24,081,324 | 18,325,297 |
| 1949-50 | 25,577,005 | 21,478,517 |
| 1950-51 | 32,044,378 | 28,899,307 |
| 1951-52 | 35,199,439 | 30,715,253 |

Evidently, in this half a century of trade between Haiti and the United States, Haitian importations from the United States constantly exceeded Haitian exportations to the United States. There were only three instances where the balance of trade was in Haiti's favor: the fiscal years of 1941-42, 1942-43, and 1944-45. This was because of World War II. The total balance in favor of Haiti was a mere $3,923,432 for these three fiscal years combined. This figure was insignificant compared to the balance in favor of the United States during the occupation, for instance. There was an average balance of over 8 million dollars in favor of the United States for each of the eighteen Haitian fiscal years during the occupation (counting from 1915-16 to 1933-34).

Haitian foreign trade with other countries followed the same pattern as that with the United States in terms of types of goods exchanged and in terms of trade balance.[6]

## HAITIAN FOREIGN TRADE (IN US DOLLARS):

| Fiscal year 1949-50 | Exportations | Importations |
|---|---|---|
| USA | $21,478,518 | $27,577,005 |
| Italy | 4,436,920 | 516,411 |
| England | 1,260,348 | 1,271,740 |
| Canada | 362,949 | 1,639,155 |
| France | 189,755 | 493,475 |
| | $27,728,490 | $31,497,786 |

| Fiscal year 1951-52 | Exportations | Importations |
|---|---|---|
| USA | $30,715,253 | $35,199,439 |
| Italy | 4,263,085 | 463,879 |
| England | 484,384 | 2,228,992 |
| Canada | 322,159 | 3,222,400 |
| France | 154,968 | 910,830 |
| Germany | 310,021 | 1,332,948 |
| | $36,249,870 | $43,358,488 |

It is evident in both sets of figures that Haitian–American trade comprised over half of Haiti's total commerce with foreign countries. Exports exceeded imports for both fiscal years only in the case of trade with Italy. As a matter of fact, the Haitian–Italian trade balance was so advantageous to Haiti that it helped upset the imbalance of Haitian commerce with the other countries; Haitian exportations even exceeding foreign importations in overall foreign trading.

Little Haitian capital was used in the acquisition of industrial machinery and tools. Haitian foreign importations were very heavy in consumer goods. In 1969, for instance, consumer goods accounted for 64.1 percent of Haiti's total imports as compared with 10.6 percent in imported capital goods for agriculture, industry, and transportation.[7] The economic development of the country was jeopardized by the scarcity of capital investment in the productive sector with almost no effort being made toward the diversification of the country's economy.

What were the prospects for economic development in Haiti? Haiti surely had some mineral resources; a good survey of its mineral deposits has yet to be taken. There used to be gold on the island. The Spaniards did such a good job extracting it that there was very little or none left by the seventeenth century. There were deposits of bauxite, copper, and salt. Small deposits of low grade coal, lignite, and manganese also existed in the country. There were speculations concerning oil deposits; the Haitian government gave a rather liberal lease for oil prospection to an American company. The only mineral ores that were exploited were bauxite and copper. These ores were extracted by foreign companies for exportation.

Haiti was deriving no substantial revenues from the exploitation of these ores. These mineral resources represented its potential for industrialization. Whereas capital and technology could somehow be obtained, mineral resources were either present or absent, and they were irreplaceable. They were "quick assets," and their mining for exportation meant the giving away of the country's potential for industrialization, unless the revenues thus generated were reinvested in industry.

The depletion of the island's natural resources, started since colonial times, continued after independence. Hàitian peasants deforested the country both to secure lumber for export and for use as fuel. The immediate effect of this deforestation was the precipitated erosion of Haiti's small portion of arable land.

The country opssessed few other important natural resources besides the land and what it could produce through agriculture. Mountains made up over two-thirds of its total area, 10,714 square miles. Four lowland areas lay amidst the mountains: 1) the Plaine du Nord around the town of Cap-Haitien in the north; 2) the Plateau Central around Hinche in the east; 3) the Plaine de l'Artibonite in the central section of the country, along the Artibonite River; and 4) the Plaine du Cul-de-Sac in the south near Port-au-Prince. The total area of these plains (including the plateau) added up to about four thousand square miles. Much of the country was semiarid. Only 23 percent of the land area was arable, or less than half an acre per person. Although no direct correlation exists between land per head and income per head, given the predominantly rural character of Haiti, the paucity of cultivatable land per capita was very significant. The antiquated agricultural methods and the decreased fertility of the soil through the years made this situation worse.

This related to the whole question of whether the country could provide enough food and employment, and whether there was sufficient economic growth to accommodate its continuously growing population. As many other underdeveloped countries with relatively large populations and high birthrates, Haiti faced the specter of famine.

In 1950, the total population amounted to 3,097,220 people. Depending upon the criteria used to delimit the urban centers from the rural areas, the rural population of the country ranged between 87.4 percent and 92.3 percent. Both the rural areas and the urban centers were densely populated. The population density of Haiti, just as its population growth rate, was among the highest in the hemisphere. There were approximately 419 persons per square mile in 1966. The density for 1970 was estimated at 450 persons per square mile. The population growth rate approximated 25 percent every twenty years.[8] The birthrate between 1959 and 1961 was 45 to 50 per 1,000 persons, and the death rate was from 20 to 25 per 1,000.[9] The 1971 census placed Haiti's population at 4,244,000, a 37 percent increase since 1950. More recent statistical data were not available.

The living conditions in Haiti compared most unfavorably to those of the other countries in the Americas. Haiti had the lowest GNP per capita among the American states. The average life expectancy was an estimated forty-five years. The infant mortality rate ranged from 170 to 200 per 1,000 live births. The country had the lowest ratio of hospital beds to persons in the American hemisphere: 70:100,000. There was about one medical doctor per 14,000 people. Two-thirds of the doctors and over 80 percent of the nurses were located in the capital, Port-au-Prince. The rural areas of Haiti, in particular, were affected by a high level of morbidity. Tuberculosis and tetanus were endemic. Malaria had not been eradicated completely. Intestinal disorders (bacterial and parasitic) were prevalent, and kwashiorkor, a protein deficiency of children, was widespread. The country's agricultural production declined both in per-capita terms and absolutely during the 1960s.

The economic state of Haiti was indeed deplorable: "Without its exports of coffee, sugar and sisal, tourism, remittances from Haitians abroad, and disguised foreign aid, Haiti's already parlous and impoverished economy would have been declared irredeemably bankrupt."[10] A number of hurricanes (Flora in 1963, Cleo in 1965, and Ines in 1966) contributed to the economic decline of the country during the 1960s. Haiti was also affected by a severe drought in 1968. The agricultural sector of the economy was the hardest hit. Losses due to these natural disasters were estimated at 50 million dollars by the government.

There were three main sectors of activities in the Haitian economy. These were the administrative and political sector, the sector of commercial activities, and the agricultural sector. The government constituted the chief source of employment for the members of the elite, while the commercial sector was almost completely in the hands of foreigners and naturalized aliens. These two sectors comprised about 10 percent or less of Haiti's total population, and their sphere of activities was concentrated in the coastal cities, especially Port-au-Prince. The economy was basically agricultural. As much as 87 percent of the total population was involved in agriculture. Agricultural products comprised about 97 percent of Haiti's total exportation to foreign markets.

Given the nature of its economy, the economic life of the nation depended heavily upon the sale of its crops on the foreign markets. The first two sectors of the economy fed upon the third. If allowance were made for an oversimplification of the Haitian economy, it would appear that the agricultural sector or close to 90 percent of the population produced approximately 90 percent of the country's exportations, thanks to which the commercial and politico-administrative sectors were able to absorb 90 percent of the importations. The continuous trade imbalance with its trading partners drained national resources and slowed the rate of capital formation and investment, which in turn hampered national economic growth. The country was caught in a vicious economic cycle that was very hard to break.

# 6

# By Way of Conclusion

Color prejudice is deeply rooted in Haiti's colonial past. In Saint-Domingue, it masked a conflict that was primarily economic in nature. The mulattoes, particularly the freedmen, stood in an exploitative relationship with the enslaved blacks. The ascendance of the slaves jeopardized their economic interests as much as those of the French colonists. This fact should provide an insight into the behavior of the freedmen in the "Suisse" Affair:

The freedmen had entered into armed conflict with the colonists during the second half of the eighteenth century. They hired 400 slave mercenaries who became known as "Suisses"—whence the name of this affair. The slaves were promised freedom upon the successful conclusion of the fight with the colonists. The battle over, the defeated colonists convinced the victorious freedmen that the Suisses constituted a threat to the colonial order and, therefore, could not go free in Saint-Domingue. Consequently, the slave mercenaries were sent in exile to Jamaica. The English colonists there also considered them a threat and thus sent them back to Saint-Domingue. French colonial authorities refused to let them back in the colony, and they were left on the pontoons in Saint-Domingue's port where they were all murdered by the colonists. No freedmen came to their aid.

Dessalines, himself a former black slave, was assassinated in 1806, two years after he gave the country its independence, because the attempted to redistribute the land of Haiti equitably between the former freedmen and the former slaves. His murder was carried out by former freedmen in his own government. The conflict between the former freedmen and the former slaves led to the division of the country into two separate and independent states from 1807 to 1820. Pétion, a mulatto and former freedman who had participated in the conspiracy against Dessalines, ruled in the south; while Christophe, a former black slave who had no part in his predecessor's murder, reigned in the north.

Haiti's social structure changed little since colonial times. Mulattoes and white foreigners dominated the country. Even when blacks won political control, the mulattoes and the white foreigners always maintained their dominance of the economy, and as such never lost complete control over the government.

Color prejudice served as a means to protect the economic interests of the elite. This is what racism did in the colony of Saint-Domingue; it fixated the economic relationship between the Europeans and the Africans. The colonial system had assured itself a permanent slave labor force as the enslaved blacks transmitted their servile status to their children. Even after the abolition of slavery, the stigma of exploitation and inferiority remained with the blacks.

The correspondence between color and class was not so clear in Haiti. Nevertheless, while blacks were found in the elite, mulattoes still predominated. President François Duvalier attempted to redistribute power and wealth between mulattoes and blacks. His social revolution caused members of the elite to flee the country. His efforts were thwarted by the lack of support from the elite, economic stagnation, and corruption. The elite still remained largely mulatto, though less so than previously.

The ability to speak French fluently was essential for upward mobility in Haitian society. The linguistic cleavage operated in a way similar to that of color prejudice. It separated the elite from the rest of the society. Monolingual Creole speakers were deprived of all the benefits that were contingent upon a knowledge of the official language. The ultimate beneficiaries of color prejudice and the linguistic problem were the neocolonial powers.

The Haitian elite became, consciously or unconsciously, a collaborator of the neocolonial powers. It was too alienated from itself and the society as a whole to serve the national interest. To the detriment of the country, it pursued its own self-interests.

The Revolution of 1803 was incomplete. Revolution not only means fundamental change in political organization but also the creation of a new socioeconomic structure, with a new cultural ideology. Haitians were still left with the task of completing what their forefathers started before 1804. The revolution should have promoted national economic development and made possible the participation of the masses in the government; it should have established democracy. The failure to restructure the society and the economy beyond the achievement of political autonomy and the abolition of slavery brought about neocolonialism and the outright occupation of the country from 1915 to 1934. The same thing could recur as these conditions repeat themselves.

The orientation of the national economy toward the world market as a supplier of raw materials and purchaser of finished goods, coupled with the inadequacy of capital investments in the productive sector, rendered the country both economically and politically vulnerable. Its economic growth was stunted, and it failed to develop the socioeconomic infrastructure crucial to its development. The bankruptcy of the government and of the whole economy invited foreign interference in Haitian affairs. The problems of economic stagnation and population growth were only partially alleviated by foreign aid and emigration.

The combination of all these social, economic, environmental, and political pressures forced Haitians to seek a future outside of their country. The members of the lower classes suffered the most from these adverse living conditions. Their desperation was recently evidenced by their pathetic exodus to the United States by rudimentary sailboats.

A Haitian solution to these problems is still possible with disinterested outside help. The temptation to apply ready-made foreign ideological formulas born out of different circumstances should be resisted at all costs. Solutions relevant to Haitian conditions are needed, and their development requires creativity and ideological originality in a climate of freedom, tolerance and cooperation. The pitfalls of racism and cultural isolationism must definitely be avoided. The design and implementation of the social, economic, and political remedies will demand tremendous effort and dedication on the part of Haitian leaders and the people as a whole. There is, first of all, need for greater political stability and better government in order to promote economic development. The economy should be diversified, for the cultivation of a few crops for export cannot constitute the basis of a viable economy. Efforts should be made to balance Haiti's foreign trade by cutting down on imports while stimulating the national economy toward self-sufficiency in areas where possible. Finally, population growth should be curbed.

# Notes

## INTRODUCTION

1. The next largest island in the Caribbean Sea after Cuba is that which is politically divided into the Republic of Haiti and the Dominican Republic. This island of 27,750 square kilometers was formerly inhabited by Amerindians who called it Haiti, meaning land of mountains. When Columbus landed there in 1492, he renamed it Hispaniola, or little Spain.

   Initially colonized by the Spaniards, France formally wrested the western portion—approximately one-third of the island—from Spain in 1697 by the Treaty of Ryswick. The French colony became known as Saint-Domingue. When Saint-Domingue achieved independence from France in 1804, the country became known as Haiti again.

   Saint-Domingue had a total population of about 520,000 around 1788 to 1789. The French colonists numbered roughly 40,000, or 8 percent of the total colonial population. There were 28,000 *affranchis* or freedmen (5 percent) and 452,000 African slaves (87 percent). The Spaniards had exterminated the indigenous population of the island within their first century of contact with them.

   The contemporary population of Haiti descended chiefly from the Africans, who were imported through the slave trade, and partly from the European colonists. Since the Haitian government did not recognize distinctions of color or race, a statistical breakdown of the current population in accordance with such criteria is not available.

## 1. THE ELITE WITHIN THE CURRENT SOCIAL STRUCTURE

1. Webster's Seventh New Collegiate Dictionary, 1967 edition, definition 1a and 1b of elite.
2. Wingfield and Parenton, 1965:339.

3. Leyburn, 1945:5, 7.
4. Price-Mars, 1940:75, 78.
5. Webster's Seventh New Collegiate Dictionary, 1967 edition, definitions of bourgeois and bourgeoisie.
6. *Ibid.*, definition of aristocracy.
7. Simpson, 1940:499.
8. Nadel, 1956:415.
9. My translation of the French, Duvalier, 1966:323, quotation of Mercier.
10. My translation of the French, Duvalier, 1966:323-324.

## 2. THE SOCIOLOGICAL ROLE OF COLOR PREFERENCES

1. The issue of racism is best understood within the context of Pierre L. Van Den Berghe's definition of race "to mean *not* a subspecies of Homo sapiens but a group of people who in a given society are socially defined as different from other groups by virtue of certain real or putative physical differences." (Van Den Berghe, 1970:10.)
2. Fanon, 1963:35-36.
3. Sartre, in Fanon, 1963:7.
4. My translation of the French, Table of Interracial Mating, Dorsinville, 1961:67.
5. Hoetink, 1967:120.
6. *Ibid.*, p. 134.
7. *Ibid.*, pp. 134-135.
8. *Ibid.*, p. 135.
9. *Ibid.*, p. 135, op. cit.
10. *Ibid.*, p. 135.
11. Van Den Berghe, 1970:21.
12. *Ibid.*, p. 38.
13. *Ibid.*, Table 1-1.
14. Simpson, 1941:648.
15. Haiti is now under a strong current of American influence through tourism and the increase in the migration of Haitians to the United States and back to their native country again.
16. Fanon, 1967:211.
17. A good book to read on this issue is *L'Héritage Colonial en Haiti*, by P. David, Madrid, 1959.
18. My translation of the French definition of "noir" (black) from the French dictionary, *Nouveau Petit Larousse*, 1969, Librairie Larousse, 17 rue du Montparnasse, et boulevard Raspail, 114. Paris VI.

19. My translation of the French definition of "blanc" (white) from the French dictionary, same as above.


## 3. LANGUAGE AND SOCIAL MOBILITY

1. Creolization refers to the development or birth of something within the colony. The people born in Saint-Domingue were called Creoles. The dialect that evolved as a result of the interaction between the French colonists and the African slaves was also named Creole. Creole is also used as a generic term to designate all languages that evolved under similar conditions.
2. Ferguson, in Hymes, 1964:435.
3. Valdman, in Schaedel, 1969:165.
4. The author was born in Port-au-Prince, Haiti. His parents were fluent in both French and Creole. His autobiographical example is merely intended to illustrate certain aspects of *diglossia* in Haiti.
5. My translation of the French, Bellegarde, 1953:66.
6. Ferguson, in Hymes, 1964:431.
7. *Ibid.*
8. My translation of the French, Morose, 1970:119.
9. My translation of the French, Bellegarde, 1953:62.
10. Fanon, 1967:18.
11. See footnote number 15, chapter on Color Prejudice.
12. Fanon, 1967:18.
13. *Ibid.*, p. 8.
14. *Ibid.*, p. 9.
15. *Ibid.*, p. 10.
16. Ferguson, in Hymes, 1964:432-433.
17. Morose, 1970:120.
18. Bull, in Hymes, 1964:528.
19. My translation of the French, Morose, 1970:125.
20. Fishman, Ferguson and Gupta, 1968:129.
21. Fanon, 1967:17-18.
22. Halliday, in Fishman, 1968:161.
23. *Ibid.*
24. My translation of the French, Morose, 1970:119-120.


## 4. THE FOREIGN INFLUENCES

1. The expression "developing countries" is a euphemism for "underdeveloped countries"; both expressions are used to refer to the nonindustrialized countries of the Third World.

2. The Third World consists of Asian, African, and Latin-American peoples.
3. Woddis, 1967:61.
4. Bellegarde, 1953:39.
5. Rotberg, 1971:111.
6. Haiti was then divided into two states: Christophe ruled as King Henry I in the northern half of the country; and Pétion presided over a republic in the south.
7. Rotberg, 1971:66-67.
8. Diederich & Burt, 1969:30.
9. *Ibid.*, pp. 31-32.
10. Moral, 1961:63, see footnote.
11. My translation of the French, *Ibid.*, p. 64.
12. My translation of the French, Dorsainvil, 1926:319.
13. Turnier, 1955:291.

## 5.   WHAT HAPPENED TO THE HAITIAN ECONOMY

1. Free people, for the most part of mixed ancestry, who were also oppressed by the colonists.
2. Hubert, 1950:14, *op. cit.*
3. Bellegarde, 1938:214.
4. CONADEP, 1970-1971.
5. Turnier, 1955:339-347.
6. Bellegarde, 1953:52-53.
7. CONADEP, 1970-1971.
8. Moral, 1959:28.
9. Collier's Encyclopedia, 1970:581.
10. Rotberg, 1971:15.

# Bibliography

Ans, Andre M. d'. *Le Créole Français d'Haïti*. Paris: Mouton, The Hague, 1968.

Ardouin, C. N. C. *Essais sur l'Histoire d'Haïti*. Port-au-Prince, Haiti, 1865.

Beauvoir, V. *Le Contrôle Financier du Gouvernement des États-Unis sur la République d'Haïti*. Paris: Recueil Sirey, 1930.

Bellegarde, Dantes. *Au Service d'Haïti*. (Autobiography.) Port-au-Prince: Imprimerie Théodore, 1962.

_____. *Haïti et ses Problèmes*. Montreal: Bernard Valiquette (no date).

_____. *Haïti et son Peuple*. Paris: Nouvelles Editions Latines, 1953.

_____. *Histoire du Peuple Haïtien, 1492-1952*. Port-au-Prince, 1953.

_____. *La Nation Haïtienne*. Paris, 1938.

Berghe, Pierre L. Van Den. *Race and Ethnicity*. New York: Basic Books, Inc., 1970.

Bottomore. T. B. *Elites and Society*. London: C. A. Watts & Co., Ltd., 1964.

Brutus, E. *Instruction Publique en Haïti, 1492-1945*. Port-au-Prince: Imprimerie de l'Etat, 1948.

Burling, R. *Man's Many Voices*. New York: Holt, Rinehart & Winston, Inc., 1970.

Cleaver, Eldridge. *Soul on Ice*. New York: McGraw-Hill, 1967, 1968.

Cook, M. "Education in Haiti," in *United States Bureau of Education Bulletin*, 1948, no. 1.

_____. *(An Introduction to) Haiti*. Department of Cultural Affairs Pan American Union, Washington, D.C., 1951.

Courlander, Harold. *The Drum and the Hoe: Life and Lore of the Haitian People*. Berkeley and Los Angeles: University of California Press, 1960.

_____, and R. Bastien. *Religion and Politics in Haiti*. ICR Studies I, Washington, D.C.: Institute for Cross-Cultural Research, 1966.

David, P. *L'Héritage Colonial en Haïti*. Madrid: LANGA Y CIA, 1959.

Denis, L. and F. Duvalier. "La Civilisation Haïtienne: Notre Men-
talité Est-Elle Africaine ou Gallo-Latine?" in *Revue de la Société
d'Histoire et de Géographie d'Haïti,* vol. VII, May 1936, pp. 1-31.
_____. *Le Problème des Classes à Travers l'Histoire d'Haïti.* Port-
au-Prince, 1958.
Diederich, B. and A. Burt. *Papa Doc: The Truth About Haiti Today.*
New York: McGraw-Hill, 1969.
Dorsainvil, J. C. *Manuel d'Histoire d'Haïti.* Procure des Frères de
l'Instruction Chrétienne. Port-au-Prince, 1926.
Dorsinville, L. *Abrégé d'Histoire d'Haïti (Seconde, Rhétorique, et
Philosophie),* vol. II. Port-au-Prince: Imprimerie de l'Etat, 1961.
Dumont, R. *False Start in Africa.* Translated from the French by
P. N. Ott. London: Andre Deutsch Limited, 1966.
Durand, R. *Regards sur la Croissance Economique d'Haïti.* Port-au-
Prince: Imprimerie des Antilles, 1965.
Duvalier, F. *Oeuvres Essentielles,* vol. I. Collection Oeuvres Essenti-
elles, 1966.
Encyclopedias: *see* "Reference books."
Faine, J. *Le Créole dans l'Univers.* Port-au-Prince: Imprimerie de
l'Etat, 1939.
_____. *Philologie Créole.* Port-au-Prince: Imprimerie de l'Etat,
1937.
Fanon, Frantz. *Black Skin, White Masks.* Translated from the French
by C. L. Markmann. New York: Grove Press, Inc., 1967.
_____. *The Wretched of the Earth.* Translated from the French by
C. Farrington. New York: Grove Press, Inc., 1963.
Fishman, J. A., ed. *Readings in the Sociology of Language.* Paris:
Mouton, The Hague, 1968. Especially the article by M. A. K.
Halliday, "The Users and Uses of Language," pp. 139-169.
_____, Charles A. Ferguson and J. Das Gupta, eds. *Language
Problems of Developing Nations.* New York: John Wiley & Sons,
Inc., 1968.
Frazier, E. Franklin. *Black Bourgeoisie.* New York: The Free Press,
Inc., a division of the Macmillan Company, 1957.
Georges-Jacob, K. *Contribution à l'Etude de l'Homme Haïtien.* Port-
au-Prince, 1946.
_____. *L'Ethnie Haïtienne.* Port-au-Prince: Imprimerie de l'Etat,
1941.
Gumperz, John J. and Hymes, Dell, eds. *Directions in Sociolinguis-
tics.* New York: Holt, Rinehart & Winston, Inc., 1972.
Hall, Robert A. *Haitian Creole.* With the collaboration of S.
Comhaire-Sylvain, H. O. McConnel and A. Métraux. Philadel-
phia: American Folklore Society, 1953.

Herskovits, Melville J. *Life in a Haitian Valley.* New York: Knopf, 1937.

Hoetink, Harry. *Caribbean Race Relations: A Study of Two Variants.* Translated from the Dutch by E. M. Hooykaas. Oxford: Oxford University Press, Institute of Race Relations, 1967.

Hubert, G. A. "Some Problems of a Colonial Economy: A Study of Economic Dualism in Haiti," in *Inter-American Economic Affairs.* Vol. III, Spring 1950, pp. 3-30.

Hurston, Zora N. *Tell My Horse.* Hurston, 1938.

Hymes, Dell, ed. *Language in Culture and Society.* New York: Harper & Row Publishers, Inc., 1964. Especially the articles in Part VII and VIII, particularly

    #41  L. Bloomfield, "Literate and Illiterate . . ." pp. 391-96.

    #45  C. A. Ferguson, "Diglossia," pp. 429-39.

    #49  W. Bright, "Social Dialect and Language . . ." pp. 469-72.

    #53  A. R. Diebold, "Incipient Bilingualism," pp. 495-510.

    #55  P. L. Garvin, "The Standard Language," pp. 521-26.

    #56  W. Bull, "The Use of the Vernacular," pp. 527-33.

    #57  J. Reinecke, "Trade Jargons and Creole . . ." pp. 534-46.

Jackson, George. *Soledad Brother: The Prison Letters of George Jackson.* New York: World Entertainers Limited, a Bantam Book, 1970.

Jahn, Janheinz. *Muntu: An Outline of the New African Culture.* Translated by M. Greene. New York: Grove Press, Inc., 1961.

Jourdain, E. *Du Français aux Parlers Créoles.* Paris, 1956.

Lasswell, Harold D. and Lerner, Daniel, et al. *The Comparative Study of Elites.* Stanford, California: Stanford University Press, Hoover Institute Studies, Series B: Elites, no. 1, January 1952.

Leyburn, James G. *The Haitian People.* New Haven: Yale University Press, 1945.

Lipset, Seymour M. and Solari, A., eds. *Elites in Latin America.* New York: Oxford University Press, 1967.

Logan, Rayford W. "Education in Haiti," in *The Journal of Negro History,* vol. XV, 1930, pp. 401-60.

_____. "Où en Sommes-Nous avec l'Élite Intellectuelle d'Haïti?" in *Journal of Inter-American Studies,* vol. III, 1961, pp. 121-32.

Métraux, Alfred. *Le Vaudou Haïtien.* Paris: Gallimard, 1958.

Millspaugh, Arthur C. *Haiti under American Control, 1915-1930.* Originally published in 1931 by World Peace Foundation, Boston. Reprinted 1970 by Negro Universities Press, a Division of Greenwood Press, Inc., Westport, Connecticut.

Mirville, S. *L'École Primaire.* Port-au-Prince, 1959.

Montague, L. L. *Haiti and the United States 1714-1938.* Durham, North Carolina: Duke University Press, 1940.

Moore, O. E. *Haiti: Its Stagnant Society and Shackled Economy.* Smithtown, New York: Exposition Press, Inc., 1972.

Moral, P. *L'Économie Haïtienne.* Port-au-Prince: Imprimerie Tel-homme, 1959.

_____. *Le Paysan Haïtien.* Paris: Maisonneuve et Larose, 1961.

Morose, J. P. *Pour une Réforme de l'Éducation en Haïti.* Thèse présenté à la Faculté des Lettres de l'Université de Fribourg en Suisse pour obtenir le grade de docteur, 1970.

Mosca, Gaetano. *The Ruling Class.* Translated by H. D. Kahn. New York and London: McGraw-Hill Book Company, Inc., 1939.

Nadel, S. F. "The Concept of Social Elites" in *International Social Science Bulletin.* vol. VIII, no. 3, 1956, pp. 413-24.

Nyerere, Julius K. *Ujamaa: Essays on Socialism.* Oxford: Oxford University Press, 1968.

Paul, E. C. *Panorama du Folklore Haïtien.* (Présence Africaine en Haïti), Port-au-Prince: Imprimerie de l'Etat, 1962.

Price-Mars, J. *De Saint-Domingue à Haïti: Essai sur la Culture, les Arts et la Littérature.* Paris: Présence Africaine, 1959.

_____. "Le Processus d'une Culture," in *Acculturation in the Americas* by Sol Tax (ed.). Chicago: The University of Chicago Press, 1952.

_____. "Social Caste and Social Problems in Haiti," in *The Inter-American Quarterly,* July 1940, vol. 2, no. 3, pp. 75-80.

Quarterly Economic Review: Cuba, Dominican Republic, Haiti, Puerto Rico. Annual Supplement 1972, The Economist Intelligence Unit Limited.

Raymond, R. J. *Du Créole au Français.* Port-au-Prince: Presses Nationales d'Haïti, 1966.

Rigaud, Milo. *La Tradition Voudou et le Voudou Haïtien.* Paris: Niclaus, 1953.

Romain, J. B. "L'Homme Haïtien: Ses Origines Ethniques, sa Psychologie," in *Congrès International des Sciences Anthropologiques et Ethnologiques,* vol. VI. Paris: Musée de l'Homme, 1960, pp. 243-46.

_____. *Quelques Moeurs et Coutumes des Paysans Haïtiens.* Port-au-Prince: Imprimerie de l'Etat, 1959.

Rotberg, Robert I. *Haiti, the Politics of Squalor.* Rotberg with C. K. Clague. The Twentieth Century Fund. Boston: Houghton Mifflin Company, 1971.

Schaedel, Richard P., ed. *Research and Resources of Haiti.* Research Institute for the Study of Man, 1969.

Simpson, G. E. "Haiti's Social Structure," in *American Sociological Review,* vol. VI, 1941, pp. 640-49.

_____. "Haitian Politics," in *Social Forces*, vol. XX, 1942, pp. 487-91.

_____. "Haitian Peasant Economy," in *Journal of Negro History*, 25(4), 1940, pp. 498-519.

Stewart, W. A. "Race and Nationality in Haiti," in *The Negro History Bulletin*, February 1958, vol. XXI, no. 5, pp. 111-12.

Sylvain, S. *Le Créole Haïtien*. Port-au-Prince: Wetteren (Belgique), 1936.

Tawney, Richard H. *Religion and the Rise of Capitalism*. New York: Harcourt, Brace and Company, 1926.

Turnier, A. *Les États-Unis et le Marché Haïtien*. Washington, D.C., 1955.

Vaissière, P., de. *Saint-Domingue: La Société et la Vie Créoles sous l'Ancien Régime (1629-1789)*. Paris, 1909.

Veblen, Thorstein B. *The Theory of the Leisure Class*. New York: The Viking Press, Inc., July 1931.

Watkins, M. H. "Race, Caste and Class in Haiti," in *The Midwest Journal*, vol. I, no. 1, Winter 1948, Lincoln University Press.

Weber, Max. *The Protestant Ethic and the Spirit of Capitalism*. Translated by T. Parsons. New York: C. Scribner's and Sons, 1930.

Wingfield, R. and V. J. Parenton. "Class Structure and Class Conflict in Haitian Society," in *Social Forces*, 43(3), 1965, pp. 338-47.

Woddis, J. *An Introduction to Neo-Colonialism*. 1967.

Worsley, Peter. *The Third World*. Chicago: The University of Chicago Press, 1964, 1967.

Young, M. de. *Man and Land in the Haitian Economy*, in Latin American Monographs Series, no. 3. Gainesville, Florida: University Presses of Florida, March 1958.

## REFERENCE BOOKS

*Collier's Encyclopedia*. 1970. Section on Haiti.
*Encyclopedia Americana*. 1971. Section on Haiti.

## REPORTS

CONADEP, Conseil National de Development et de Planification, Republique d'Haïti. *Plan d'Action Economique et Sociale, 1970-1971*.

*Report of the United States Commission on Education in Haiti*. October 1, 1930. United States Government Printing Office, Washington, D.C., 1931.